תפרק מצי עול ומישד לי עדלה

זכור ה

פכפר ירדך איש וזר יהכהה
מיור אבכעשין עבירת זר
זמס בלב הייוה לאה לאבזר

זכור ג

נהעילל ברבע כאשה
יהין לפי השיאר פאשה
התי בפריו היוה כלב אשה

זכור ז

רע מירעים נתעב ונאלה
חלק להשהית ולומר האה
טמטי גאים פה להובל אה

זכור ה

נט מנו עמלסי
טס כילק לאבר הלקי ירוע
פכורים לעין כל בלוקסי

זכור ט

פש מהערימ יה ירד רכת
עמי ער הרמיה במדכז
חויב הוא להוריב מיה

זכור כ

רשב נאב בלי עול בירד בסיג
מלשון שנה היות מלך ערד
לשבות שבי מירד והרד

זכור נ

כיל שנה באולהי להשהנה
מידז בעלותי מיהר
ירושת וגלה נבלותי

זכור ל

קעסע בצתי משורש מלשוב

SMOKE AND ASHES

THE STORY OF THE HOLOCAUST

Revised & Expanded Edition

BY BARBARA ROGASKY

Holiday House, Inc./New York

The title of this book comes from *In the City of Slaughter*, by Chaim Nachman Bialik, a long poem published in 1905 about the great 1903 pogrom in Kishinev, Russia. Two verses appear in *The Holocaust Kingdom: A Memoir*, by Alexander Donat (New York: The Holocaust Library, 1978), p. 99. They are reprinted on page iv by permission of the publishers.

Library of Congress Cataloging-in-Publication Data

Rogasky, Barbara.
Smoke and ashes: the story of the Holocaust / Barbara Rogasky—
Rev. and expanded ed. • p. cm.
Includes bibliographical references and index. • ISBN 0-8234-1612-7 (hardcover)
1. Holocaust, Jewish (1939–1945)—Juvenile literature. [1. Holocaust, Jewish (1939–1945)] I. Title. • D804.3. R64 2001 • 940.53'18—dc21   2001016797
ISBN 0-8234-1677-1 (pbk.)

The endpapers are from a song in a Hebrew holiday prayer book, folios 43a and 43b, Germany, 1380. The song, "Zochar" (Remember), lists the historical persecutions of the Jews and asks God to remember those events. This copy of the prayer book was written by hand on vellum. It is preserved in the Dorot Jewish Division, The New York Public Library, Astor, Lenox and Tilden Foundations.

Book design by Stephanie Bart-Horvath

Maps on pages 54, 55, and 124 by Heather Saunders

For the Six Million

The first edition of this book was finished several years ago. Then, and only then, I learned from my older sister a fact that had been kept from me as a child.

Over fifty members of my family had been murdered in Russia during the years of the Holocaust.

To the family I never knew, and now will never know:

This edition of *Smoke and Ashes* is dedicated to you.

Only a lost people can lament so:
Smoke and ashes—that is its soul,
And its heart a desert wilderness,
Without an ounce of anger or revenge.

✦ ✦ ✦

Where is the fist that shall smite?
Where is the thunderbolt to revenge?
To shake the world and rend the sky?
To overthrow My seat, My throne?

—CHAIM NACHMAN BIALIK
From *In the City of Slaughter*

CONTENTS

ACKNOWLEDGMENTS TO THE FIRST EDITION

Several people and organizations have been especially helpful to me in putting *Smoke and Ashes* together. I want to thank them here.

Bonnie Gurewitsch of the Center for Holocaust Studies, Brooklyn, New York. Marek Web of the YIVO Institute for Jewish Research, New York. Judith Levine of Yad Vashem, Jerusalem, Israel. Diane Spielman of the Leo Baeck Institute, New York. Ann Cassouto of Shapolsky Publishers, New York.

I owe a debt of both personal and professional gratitude to these: Jean K. Aull of Open Fields School, Thetford, Vermont, who listened to my voice for many tedious hours. Robert Gere of Sun Photo, Hanover, New Hampshire, who managed to produce copies of photographs when all seemed lost. Marilyn M. Houston, whose efficiency and humor saved hours of work and possibly my physical and mental health as well. Terry Viens, who deciphered the indecipherable. Margery Cuyler, my editor at Holiday House, who believed I could do it in the first place. And to Trina Hyman, who managed to make it through rather well, all things considered.

Last, for many reasons not to be explained, to my mother and father, whose *Yiddishkeit* and memory made it necessary for me to write this book.

Barbara Rogasky
Lyme, New Hampshire

ACKNOWLEDGMENTS TO THE REVISED EDITION

Gratitude and appreciation for their helpfulness beyond the purely professional to: Chris Sims, United States Holocaust Memorial Museum, Washington, D.C.; Fama Mor, the Simon Wiesenthal Foundation, Los Angeles, California; Jessica Singer, YIVO Institute for Jewish Research, New York, New York.

Julia Kühn and Alfred Posener, editor and translator respectively of the German edition (*Der Holocaust*, Rowholt-Berlin, 1999), demanded such clarity and accuracy from me that it helped focus and clarify my thinking for this edition. And so, in English: Thank you, again.

Particular gratitude to Ruth Segal of Hanover, New Hampshire. Her stories of Poland before the war, of her escape to safety, and of her family, all of whom perished in the Holocaust, gave history the life and sadness that books cannot supply. Her generosity in lending me her husband's safe-conduct visa took a certain courage, and for that I am especially grateful.

A special debt is owed to Regina Griffin, editor-in-chief and vice president at Holiday House, Inc., whose patience with endless delays was a miracle of publishing, if not of nature, as were her confidence, optimism and encouragement.

A personal thank-you to Bobby Fletcher and Eugene Tchana, for preventing me from taking a cleaver to my computer.

Lastly, to George, whose sweet temper and constancy helped me get through each day, in more ways than he can understand.

Needless to say, the responsibility for any inaccuracies or errors lies with me alone.

Barbara Rogasky
Thetford Hill, Vermont

SOME THINGS YOU SHOULD KNOW

This book was not written to give you nightmares.

It is about terrible things, the kinds of things that appear in nightmares. Unlike a bad dream, this really happened, and it went on happening for years.

To say the truth straight out, this is a book about murder.

In twelve years, almost six million people were deliberately murdered. Six million, enough to fill the city of Philadelphia over three times or Dallas more than five.

They were not killed because they were soldiers, nor because they were spies. They did not have a trial in which a judge and jury found them guilty of some awful crime. It made no difference whether they were men or women, old or young—one and a half million children under fifteen were among them.

They were killed because they were Jews. That was the only reason.

No special invention, no atomic or biological weapon did this. Men and women, like the men and women they killed, made this happen.

It was the period of the Holocaust, the time when the Nazis ruled Germany and Germany ruled most of Europe. They wanted a Europe that was *Judenfrei*—free of Jews. They almost succeeded.

They called their killing of millions of Jews "The Final Solution of the Jewish Question." If they had not been stopped by the armed forces of the free world, they would have unleashed their murderous madness everywhere on the face of the earth.

How did it happen and why? What did they do? Couldn't anyone stop it? How could the Jews let it happen—why didn't they fight back? Did it happen to anyone else?

This book tries to answer those questions and many more besides. But before you turn to chapter 1, there are some things you should know about the time when the Holocaust occurred.

The Nazis came to power in Germany under the leadership of Adolf Hitler in 1933. By 1939, they had started World War II, and all of Europe and Great Britain were involved in a battle for their existence. In December 1941, the United States joined the fight.

Germany had two important allies—Japan and Italy. Japan was the major power in the Far East. It was busy fighting its own wars there and in the Pacific Ocean and did not get involved with carrying out the Final Solution—perhaps because there were almost no Jews in Japan.

Italy was a dictatorship, just as Germany was. Its government, called fascist, had been in power several years before the Nazis took over in Germany. Although Italy certainly was not free from Nazi influence, it did not play an important part in Hitler's Europe and did not murder its Jews.

The United States, Great Britain and the Soviet Union made up three of the four Allied powers. France, although it had surrendered to Germany, was the fourth. Leaders who had left the country set up a government in exile in London, which represented what was called Free France. Though part of the Allied fight against Hitler, Free France had little effect on the war.

Germany attacked the Soviet Union, also called Russia, in June 1941. Until Russia's armies succeeded in turning the tide, millions of its people died in the battles against Germany. Through most of the war Russia remained suspicious of the three other Allies, and the three never lost their suspicion of Russia. Russia never admitted that the Jews were being killed just because they were Jews. It insisted that as Soviet citizens, Jews suffered as Russians, not in any particular way because they were Jews. To separate them, even by name, was not possible. The Russians would not discuss the problem.

Israel did not exist. Palestine, as the area was called then, was under British control, and had been since it acquired the area in World War I. For reasons that do not need to be explained here, Palestine was declared the Jewish National Home in 1917. Even though it was not an independent nation, Jews from other countries were allowed to settle there.

This was the background for the Nazis' years in power—1933 to 1945—the years of the Holocaust.

The word *holocaust* originally meant an offering to God that was entirely consumed by fire. It now refers to any large area or great number of people destroyed by fire. Spelled with a capital letter, it is the period during which six million of the Jews of Europe were killed, and most of their bodies burned—consumed by fire.

Reading about it is not easy. The figures are large and there are many of them. The details are unpleasant and cruel, perhaps even painful to read. But the story cannot be made pretty, like a tale told to little children. There is no happy ending.

The war took millions of lives all over the world, not only Jews. Yet this is a story of their destruction, because only they were marked for extermination. Elie Wiesel, perhaps the most famous survivor and writer of the Holocaust, said it all when he wrote: "Not all of the victims were Jewish, but all of the Jews were victims."

This book was not written to give you nightmares. But it is about the time that a nightmare came true.

ABOUT THE PHOTOGRAPHS

Several of the photographs are dark or unclear. That is because of their age—some are sixty years old or more—and also because they have been printed many times over after the original copy, which often cannot be found.

An important fact to remember is that almost all photographs of Jews in ghettos, camps and elsewhere were taken by SS or German soldiers, or by German news photographers, as the Holocaust was being carried out.

A FEW DEFINITIONS

Most important terms are explained in the book when they are used. A few are listed here to make their definitions easy to find.

Allies: The four most important nations joined in the fight against the Axis nations during World War II—the United States, Great Britain, France and the Soviet Union.

Aryan: Certain kinds of languages spoken in some parts of the world; also refers to people mostly in northern Europe who are often tall, blond and blue-eyed. Hitler and his followers believed Aryans were a superior or "master race," and that Germans were the best example. There is no such thing as an Aryan race, but that did not change their belief.

Axis: The three important enemy nations of World War II—Germany, Japan and Italy.

"Canada": The three large warehouses in Auschwitz that held the clothes and belongings of the Jews who had been gassed. The exact reason for its name is unknown, but it was called "Canada" by both prisoners and guards.

Concentration Camp: A prison camp where the Nazis sent people they thought were dangerous; "concentrated" in this way, the prisoners could do no harm. A huge number of these camps existed, big and small, throughout Germany and Nazi-controlled Europe; over six thousand operated in Poland alone. Millions of people lived, suffered and died in them. Officially the inmates were supposed to be used as labor, but living conditions and the sadistic brutality of those who ran the camps made survival very difficult.

Jews made up the largest single group imprisoned in them. They were not expected to survive; that was a deliberate Nazi policy. Auschwitz, the largest camp, was both a concentration camp and a death camp; Auschwitz I was the concentration camp. All camps were under the supervision of the SS.

Death Camp: A camp whose basic purpose was to kill Jews. Gas chambers were built especially for that use. There were six death camps, all in Poland. Auschwitz, the largest, was both a death camp and a concentration camp; the killing section was called Auschwitz II or Birkenau. All camps were under the supervision of the SS.

Einsatzgruppen: Special Action Groups. These firing squads followed the victorious German army through Eastern Europe and parts of Russia, executing Jews wherever they were found.

Final Solution: The Nazi plan to murder by gassing and any other means all the Jews of Europe. The full name is written "The Final Solution of the Jewish Question."

Führer: German word for leader or chief. As *Der Führer,* the supreme leader of Nazi Germany, Adolf Hitler.

General Government: The name given by the Germans to Nazi-occupied Poland.

Genocide: The deliberate and systematic destruction of an entire people who belong to one racial, political, cultural or religious group.

Gestapo: Abbreviation for the German words *Geheime Staatspolizei,* the Nazi State Secret Police. They arrested, jailed and tortured untold thousands during the years of the Third Reich.

Holocaust: The slaughter of approximately six million Jews by Nazi Germany and its friends, 1933 to 1945.

Kapo: The leader of a concentration camp work group who was also a prisoner.

Nazi: Abbreviation for *Nazionalsozialistische Deutsche Arbeiterpartei*, translated as the National Socialist German Workers' Party—the Nazis. The government of Germany and the only political party allowed from 1933 to 1945. No opposition was permitted on pain of imprisonment or death.

Ordnungspolizei: Order Police. The uniformed police of the Third Reich, whose major role during the war was to assist the Special Action Groups and to aid in the carrying out of the Final Solution.

Pogrom: A brief, planned, surprise attack against a defenseless Jewish community.

Reich Security Main Office: The Gestapo (Secret Police), Criminal Police and Security Service (SD) combined. It was extremely powerful. Its chief, Reinhard Heydrich, was the main designer of the Final Solution.

Russia: See Soviet Union.

SA: Abbreviation for the German word *Sturmabteilung*, meaning Storm Troopers. A private Nazi army separate from the regular German army. Its members were average Germans. They had very little power after the early years of Nazi rule. They were called "Brownshirts" because of the color of their uniforms.

SD: Abbreviation for the German word *Sicherheitsdienst*, meaning Security Service. Together with the Gestapo (Secret Police) and the Criminal Police, it formed the Reich Security Main Office.

Sonderkommando: "Special commando" in English. The Jews temporarily spared to work in the death camps' killing centers. Eventually they too were murdered and replaced by new arrivals.

Soviet Union: The Union of Soviet Socialist Republics (USSR), also called Russia. It was made up of fifteen countries or republics—including Ukraine,

Latvia, Lithuania and Estonia—united under the leadership of Russia, its major republic. The largest country in the world, with a 1989 population of 286,731,100. In 1991, the Soviet Union ceased to exist. Its former republics became a loosely connected collection of independent states and Russia itself became its own nation.

SS: Abbreviation for the German word *Schutzstaffel*, meaning Protection Squad. The SS began as Hitler's bodyguard, became a private Nazi army separate from the regular German army, and grew into the most powerful organization in the Third Reich. Its members were given special training and were considered among the best in the nation. The Death's Head Brigade, whose members wore a skull and crossbones on their caps and collars, ran the concentration camps.

Swastika: An ancient symbol, dating back about six thousand years, it often meant good luck. With some small changes, the swastika was the symbol for Nazism and became part of the German flag.

Third Reich: The German word *Reich* means Empire. According to the Nazis, the First Reich was the period of Germany's greatest power, the Holy Roman Empire, from 962 to 1806. The Second Reich was its next period of great power, beginning under the leadership of Chancellor Otto von Bismarck, from 1871 to 1890, and lasting to the end of World War I, in 1918. Hitler's Third Reich, supposed to last a "thousand years," lasted for twelve—1933 to 1945.

The 1614 attack on the ghetto in Frankfurt, Germany. The entire Jewish community was forced to leave the city. During much of the 1600s, Jews had to wear a small circle sewn on their clothes as the "Jewish badge" of identity. It can be seen on several of the figures.

I

THE ROOTS

Their synagogues should be set on fire. . . . Their
homes should likewise be broken down and destroyed.
. . . Let us drive them out of the country for all time.
—Martin Luther, 1543

When Jewish blood spurts from the knife, then things
go twice as well.
—From the fighting song of the SA

THE SEEDS OF MISUNDERSTANDING, IGNORANCE AND HATE were sown long
before Hitler. The Nazis would not have been able to succeed in their work
of destruction if the foundation had not been formed centuries earlier.

In the early years of Christianity and long into modern times, Jews were
called Christ killers, murderers of God. That crime was so basic and horrible that they were believed capable of anything and everything evil. Martin
Luther, the founder of Protestantism, declared they were the Christians'
most vicious enemy, second only to Satan himself. In the Middle Ages they
were said to have poisoned the wells and caused the years of the plague that
killed millions in Europe. Jews were believed to murder Christians, especially innocent children, in order to use their blood during religious ceremonies. This was the infamous Blood Libel, which the Nazis made good use
of again hundreds of years later.

Thus the Jews rarely lived in peace for long. Whole communities were
raided, ransacked and destroyed. Jewish children were taken from their parents to be raised as Christians. Jews were burned at the stake because they
refused to give up their religion.

Strict limits were placed on what they could and could not do. At one
time or another throughout history they were forbidden to be doctors,
lawyers or teachers of non-Jews. They were not permitted to sell food to
Christians or to hire Christians to work for them. They could not be cared

for by Christian nurses. They were not allowed to live in the same houses as non-Jews. They were forced to wear a special article of clothing or a cloth badge so that all would know they were Jews and more easily avoid them.

Christians believed that lending money and charging interest—usury—was a sin. Jews came to fill an important need by taking on that job and making money available to non-Jews who requested it. The role expanded over the years, and Jews were used by those in power to collect taxes, supervise the peasant farmers of large estates, and act as a bridge between the ruling nobility and the people in matters of money and finance. It is probably the basis in history for such ideas as "All Jews are rich" and "The Jews control all the money."

Jews were expelled from country after country, among them England, France, Spain, Portugal, Italy and Germany. When they were not expelled, they often had to live in limited special areas—the ghettos. In Russia during the late 1700s, they were restricted to a land area in the west of the country called the Pale of Jewish Settlement. The restriction was not lifted until almost two hundred years later, in the twentieth century.

Things did not improve very much closer to modern times. In Russia, Ukraine and Romania, hundreds of Jews died in pogroms in which organized groups attacked defenseless Jewish communities, looted and destroyed them, and killed or maimed their inhabitants. Between 1900 and 1904, at least 50,000 Jewish lives were lost in such incidents.

ANTI-SEMITISM IN GERMANY

The roots of anti-Semitism in Germany go back a very long time. In the eleventh century, when the Christian knights went on their crusades "For the Sake of the Cross" to convert or kill—mostly kill—the Muslims of the Middle East, they found easier victims closer to home. Thousands of Jews in German towns were massacred at the hands of German Christian Crusaders. In the fourteenth century during the years of the plague, over two hundred Jewish communities were partly or completely destroyed. Throughout their history in that country, Jews found their homes attacked, their cemeteries desecrated and their synagogues burned. Their lives were made miserable even in small ways—in many country villages it was the custom to stone Jews during the Holy Week before Easter.

Many fiercely nationalistic and anti-Semitic political parties appeared in Germany after World War I was lost, all seeking to fix blame. This election flyer from the National People's Party is typical. The headline reads, THE JEWS— GERMANY'S VAMPIRES! *It goes on to say that Jews were "the only ones to profit from the war," that Germany has signed "the most disgraceful armistice ever." It asks, "Who do we have to blame for this? The Jews!" Such parties eventually joined with the Nazis.*

In the 1800s signs of what would become the building blocks of Nazism began to appear. Anti-Jewish incidents grew in number and violence, including riots led by a group that had as its slogan, "Death and destruction to all Jews!"

But one of the most important events was the invention of the term *anti-Semitism* itself in 1873. It was used for the first time in a small book—which became very popular—called *The Triumph of Jewry Over Germanism*, by Wilhelm Marr. That marked an important change in the history of Jewish persecution.

Before then, Jews were considered dangerous because of their religion; they were capable of all things evil because of what they believed, not because of what they were. That meant it was possible for them to change for the better. The best way to show that change was to give up their religion and convert to Christianity. In other words, they could choose not to be Jews.

But after 1873 things began to be different. Now called Semites, not just Jews, they were thought of as a race for the first time. The "Jewish question" became one of birth and blood, not belief. If the Jews were a race by birth, then they could not change. From the beginning, they were basically and deeply different from everyone else. That single idea was the cornerstone of Nazi anti-Semitism.

In 1890 an "Anti-Semites' Petition" with 225,000 signatures was sent to the leader of the country demanding that Jews be removed from government, that no more Jews be allowed to come to Germany, and in general urging "the liberation of Germany from the exploitation of the Jews." The demands were not met, but the chancellor sympathized.

Anti-Semitic politicians were elected to the Reichstag, Germany's ruling body. One of them gave a speech to much applause that said such things as, "The Jews are indeed beasts of prey. . . . The Jews operate like parasites. . . . The Jews are cholera germs." Anti-Semitism was called "the greatest national progress of this century."

Anti-Jewish books and pamphlets appeared by the dozen and were read by everyone. *The Handbook of Antisemitism*, for example, went into thirty-six printings and had thousands of readers. The thousand-page *Foundations of the Nineteenth Century*, which came out in 1899, proclaimed that all the good in civilization came from the Aryans. The best true living examples of this blond and blue-eyed master race were the Germans. Most of what was bad came from their enemy, the Jews. Obviously, Hitler was influenced by these ideas, as were millions of others.

In 1903 *The Protocols of the Elders of Zion* made its appearance in Russia. It was supposed to be the secret plan of the "international Jewish conspiracy" to take over the world. Translated into many languages, it reached millions of readers everywhere. The German version appeared in 1919. By the end of the year, 120,000 copies had been sold—a huge number for that time—and classes and evening lectures were held to enlighten the public about its true meaning.

In 1921 it was proved a forgery—lies from start to finish—but that made no difference. Its popularity kept on growing, and it continued to be used as proof of the Jews' true intentions. Hitler was so impressed by *The Protocols* that he declared the Nazis could learn a lot about gaining power from its contents.

ADOLF HITLER AND *MEIN KAMPF*

Adolf Hitler was born in 1889 in Austria and went to Germany in 1913. He served in the German army in the First World War and was wounded twice. When Germany lost the war, Hitler returned to find his adopted country in turmoil.

Unemployment was extremely high. There were bloody street fights and revolutions. The government seemed unable to govern, and the country could not find its balance. Bitter, poor, hungry and angry, the people tried to find answers and fix blame for the world that seemed to be falling apart around them.

Dozens of new political organizations and parties appeared, each claiming to know the answers and to offer solutions. Most of these groups were extremely patriotic, antidemocratic, antigovernment and anti-Semitic.

Hitler was among their members. He joined a small group called the German Workers' Party that eventually became the National Socialist German Workers' Party. In German, it was the *Nationalsozialistische Deutsche Arbeiterpartei*—the Nazi party.

Helped by Hitler's magnetic personality and his amazing ability as a speaker, the party grew. Its program promised jobs, food and education to all Germans. It demanded that Germany be allowed to take its rightful strong place among the nations of the world. It "explained" that Germany had lost World War I through a "stab in the back" from its own government, which had allied itself with Jews. The Jews had so weakened the government that it had lost the will and the strength to fight.

Point Four of the Nazi party program said plainly: "Only a racial comrade can be a citizen. Only a person of German blood can be a racial comrade. No Jew, therefore, can be a racial comrade." In other words, because a Jew was a member of a different race from the Germans, he could not be a citizen of Germany. The Nazis made good on that statement a few years later.

Adolf Hitler.

In 1923, just five years after the country lost the war, an inflation hit that was the worst the world had ever seen. Millions of people were without work, but even if they had jobs there was little they could afford to buy. The German reichsmark, their unit of money, had almost no value. A loaf of bread cost five million reichsmarks. That was in the morning. The inflation grew so fast it might cost twice that in the evening. One American cent was worth 1.66 million reichsmarks. Money was carried in boxes, bags and wheelbarrows; it was not worth the paper it was printed on. Germany was simply falling apart.

Hitler and the young Nazi party tried to take over the government during this period. They failed, and Hitler was arrested. Given a five-year sentence, he spent only nine months in jail. He used that time to write the book that would become a bible of the Nazi movement—*Mein Kampf*, My Struggle. It is the story of his early years, his political development and the growth of the Nazi party.

Mein Kampf is deadly dull; it is almost impossible to read. That may explain why almost no one bothered to find out what it said. It very clearly states Nazi theories and plans for the future that would become all too real a few years later. The ideas

Hermann Goering, the number-two man in Germany. He was a drug addict, thief, and became grossly fat, but he was loved by the German people for his vicious sense of humor and his obvious enjoyment of food and drink.

that gave rise to the Holocaust are spelled out in no uncertain terms.

Hitler was possessed by the idea of race. He believed that all that was worthwhile in the world, even civilization itself, was the product of one race—the Aryan. But there is no such thing as an Aryan race. The word *Aryan* refers to certain languages spoken in some parts of the world, or to

Joseph Goebbels, Minister of Public Enlightenment and Propaganda. Everything printed in Germany had to pass his censorship; so did movies, plays and all the arts. He determined what the German people were told about Hitler, the war and the Jews. A magnificent speaking voice and great acting ability made him the most popular of Nazi speakers except for Hitler.

people mostly in northern Europe who tend to be tall, blond and blue-eyed. It is not a race. But that made no difference to Hitler or his followers. He insisted that every government and state has the sacred right and duty to protect the race and "to see to it that the blood is preserved pure." Because, he said, "All that is not race is trash."

The Jew is mentioned again and again in *Mein Kampf*.

"The Jew forms the strongest contrast to the Aryan."

"The Jewish people is without a true culture."

"The fake culture the Jew possesses is the property of other people."

The Jew is a "maggot," "parasite," "vermin," "plague," "spider sucking blood," "vampire," "pimp," "snake"—and that is far from all he said.

The Jew is everyone's enemy. He desires the "lowering of the racial level of the noblest." He wants to dominate "through extermination" the best in the nation, and replace them with "members of his own nation."

Jews disguise their true purpose by pretending to be a religion, which is "the first and greatest lie." They were "always a people with definite racial qualities, never a religion."

If the Jew is victorious, "then his crown will be the wreath on the grave of mankind, then this planet will, as it did millions of years ago, move empty through space."

Small wonder he could then say, "In fighting off the Jew, I am fighting the Lord's work."

The country had lost the war, he reminded his readers, because Germany had been weakened by not keeping itself pure; the people had been betrayed. "World War I might not have been lost," he said, "if some twelve or fifteen thousand of the Hebrew corrupters of the people had been poisoned by gas before or during the war."

The Holocaust stands as history's evidence that he meant every word he said.

2

THE NAZIS
AND THE JEWS OF GERMANY

We love Adolf Hitler, because we believe, with a faith that is deep and unshakable, that he was sent to us by God to save Germany.

—Field Marshall Hermann Goering, chosen by Hitler to be his successor

Hatred, burning hatred—that is what we want to pour into the souls of our millions of fellow Germans until the flame of rage ignites our Germany and avenges the corrupters of our nation.

—Adolf Hitler

THE NAZI PARTY GREW IN SIZE AND POPULARITY. A good part of its appeal lay in the party program. In simple, direct language it offered a defeated people a way to restore its pride. The party found a reason for the lost war and named the chief enemy of its people and way of life: the Jews.

But it was probably Hitler who did the most to bring people to the Nazi party. He had the ability as a speaker not only to make the most complicated things sound simple—any good politician can do that—but he also controlled his audiences like a master puppeteer holding invisible strings. They laughed, they cried, they turned angry, got to their feet and shouted—they did whatever the man with the penetrating blue eyes and small mustache wanted them to do.

It is almost impossible to imagine this today. Recordings of his speeches simply sound like someone close to insanity growling or shouting at top speed. But at the time, he had a truly amazing effect.

He presented himself as the one man with the answers, Germany's chosen leader—but the people also saw him as one of their own. The quotation that follows gives some idea of Hitler's effect on the masses of the German

Hitler was adored by the German people. Their joy at the sight of him was genuine and deep. Men and women cried when he appeared.

people. These are the words of an SA lieutenant named George Zeidler, who joined the Nazi party during its early years:

"Hitler, you're our man. You talk like a human being . . . who's been through the same mess we were, and not in some soft berth. You are pleading, with all your being, with all your burning heart, for us, the Germans. You want what is best for Germany because you can do no other, because it is the way you must act out of your most profound conviction as a man of decency and honor.

"He who has once looked into Hitler's eyes, he who has once heard him, will never get away from him again."

HITLER IN POWER

Over a period of a few years the Nazi party got enough votes so that the government had to take it seriously and offer it official power. Believing that

Hitler and the Nazis were like any other political group, and thinking they could be controlled, the government appointed Hitler chancellor of Germany on January 30, 1933.

The government was wrong. Within a year and a half Hitler had taken absolute power for himself, and the Nazi party ran the country.

It is likely that Hitler was clear in his desire to exterminate the Jews from the very beginning. But this could not be done all at once, nor could the steps leading to it be done openly. If the Nazis were to accomplish many of their aims, and that certainly included ridding Germany of Jews, it was necessary first to take complete control of the country. But something existed that could stop that from happening: the law.

Children were taught from their earliest years to stay away from "the evil Jew." Here is a popular children's game called "Get the Jews Out!" By throwing dice, the winner manages to get six Jews out of their homes and businesses—the circles—and on the road to Palestine. The game sold over a million copies in 1938, when Nazi policy was to force Jews to emigrate.

Carefully planned mass meetings and parades of the new Germany's armed strength restored the people's pride, eventually at the expense of most of Europe and of six million Jews.

Like every civilized country, Germany had a constitution and laws that protected the rights of its citizens. So almost as soon as Hitler was appointed chancellor, the Nazis made their complete control of Germany legally possible. They changed the laws.

Within two months of Hitler's appointment, the Nazi-controlled Reichstag passed the Emergency Decree, "For the Protection of the People and the State." All civil rights—free speech, freedom of the press, the right to assemble, the privacy of the mails—were suspended. It meant that the

All Germans between ages ten and eighteen were required by law to join the Hitler Youth—both boys and girls. Hitler said, "[I] will mold a youth from which the world will shrink in terror. I want a brutal, domineering, fearless, and cruel youth. . . ."

government—Hitler and leading Nazis—was free to do just about whatever it wanted to those who disagreed with it. The decree certainly meant that all open opposition to the Nazi party came to an end.

Next was the Enabling Act one month later, called "The Law for Terminating the Suffering of the People and Nation." With the pretext of restoring a sick Germany to health, the act enabled the government to pass any law, write any decree, perform almost any act it wished to, even if it violated the constitution. The act supplied the legal backing for dictatorship. Hitler and the Nazis never worried about laws and the rights of citizens again.

It immediately became possible to arrest opponents of the regime and lock them up for reasons of "protective custody" or "preventive detention." The first concentration camp, Dachau, was opened to hold them. No charges had to be filed against them, no warrant for their arrest was necessary, no real evidence was required. Some were killed as they were arrested "for resisting arrest" or "trying to escape." Known opponents of the regime were sure to be imprisoned, but a reputation for disagreement was enough, as was the pointed finger of a neighbor with some grudge.

A great many Jews were among them. They were opponents without question. They were not Germans, they were Jews. To the anti-Semitism of the Nazis, they were automatically "enemies of the people and the state."

Now rulers of the country, the Nazis unleashed their anti-Semitism everywhere. Throughout Germany, Jews were attacked and severely beaten; several were killed. Jewish shops and stores were broken into and vandalized. When this was brought to the attention of Hermann Goering, the man chosen by Hitler to be his successor, he said, "I will ruthlessly set the police at work wherever harm is being done to the German people. But I refuse to make the police guardians of Jewish department stores."

Thus in a little less than three months, lawlessness was in complete control in Germany—and all of it under the name of the law.

These events did not escape the world's notice, most of it very critical. When the attacks against Jews became more widespread, an unofficial boycott of German goods began, especially in the United States. The refusal of individuals and some major businesses to buy anything made in Germany had little effect. But it did seem to get the Nazis angry.

THE BOYCOTT

In reaction, Hitler called for a boycott of all Jewish businesses in Germany. It was necessary, he said, to control and give an outlet to the spontaneous acts of anti-Semitism occurring throughout the country. This was absolute nonsense, of course. The truth was that the Nazis believed the worldwide outrage at events in Germany was created by the Jews. "International Jewry," they declared, was responsible for the "atrocity propaganda" about the Jews in Germany. Joseph Goebbels, master of the Reich press, radio and propaganda, said of the boycott, "Perhaps the foreign Jews will think better of the matter when their racial comrades in Germany get it in the neck."

Preparations for the boycott were well publicized. Posters went up throughout the country, announcements appeared in all newspapers, demonstrations were held. "Germans! Defend Yourselves! Do Not Buy from Jews!" "Anyone Who Buys From Jews Is a Traitor!"

The boycott took place on April 1, 1933. Two SS men in their black uniforms and two storm troopers stood before each Jewish shop. The word *Jude*—Jew—was painted across windows, or *Juda verrecke!*—Jews perish!—a favorite Nazi slogan.

The boycott lasted just one day. It attracted attention around the world, all of it negative. It had little effect on Germany, except to frighten and worry German Jews even more.

But it did stimulate anti-Semitic feeling around the country to new heights. Individual acts of violence against Jews, their shops, homes and synagogues grew in number.

The Nazis moved quickly. On April 7, the first anti-Jewish law was passed. It was called the "Law for the Restoration of the Civil Service," usually referred to as the Aryan Law. All non-Aryans in the civil service were to be expelled. A "non-Aryan," which meant a Jew, was defined at first as anyone who had Jewish parents or two or more Jewish grandparents. Four days later, the law was changed—not for the last time—to say a non-Aryan was anyone "descended from one Jewish parent or grandparent."

Between that date and the end of the year, anti-Jewish laws affected all Jews in almost all the professions.

Jews were kept out of work in the theater, in the movies and in the arts and literature. They could not practice law in German courts. Jewish doctors and dentists were expelled from German hospitals and institutions. They were fired from newspapers and magazines, removed from the staffs of schools and universities.

Hitler said it, and the Nazis repeated it endlessly, that the Jews dominated Germany. The German people seemed to believe this as a fact, and all these laws and more were carried out ruthlessly everywhere. But the truth is different. Jews made up less than one percent of the entire population.

The Nazi fever spread. On May 10, Berlin University students decided

The boycott of Jewish-owned businesses on April 1, 1933, lasted for one day. It was not successful, but violence against Jews increased.

on an act "against the un-German spirit." They collected the works of "undesirable writers" and threw them on a huge bonfire. They burned 70,000 tons of books before they were done.

Joseph Goebbels made a speech at the scene. "The age of extreme Jewish intellectualism is now ended," he announced. "Brightened by these flames our vow shall be: The Reich and the Nation and our Führer Adolf Hitler!

Books of the "un-German spirit" were burned by students throughout Germany. In Berlin alone, 70,000 tons of books were destroyed.

Heil! Heil! Heil!"

Works of the "un-German spirit" were removed from libraries all over the country. Before it was finished, one-third of all the library books in Germany were destroyed.

One hundred years earlier, the great German poet Heinrich Heine seemed to see the future when he said:

"That was only a prelude. When they burn books, in the end it is human beings that they burn."

THE NUREMBERG LAWS

Hitler pulled his power together over the next year, often by simply killing off those who challenged him in any way. Individual acts of violence and vandalism against Jews went on, but for those few months the government added nothing new to their burdens.

On September 15, 1935, any hope that the worst was past vanished forever.

The Nuremberg Laws were passed. They were in two parts. One was called "The Law for the Protection of German Blood and German Honor"; the second, "The Reich Citizenship Law."

First, the Protection Law:

"Marriages between Jews and citizens of German or related blood are forbidden. Marriages performed despite this ban are invalid, even if performed abroad to avoid this law."

"Sexual relations between Jews and citizens of German or related blood are forbidden."

"Jews may not employ in their households female citizens of German or related blood under 45 years old."

"Jews are not permitted to display the German flag or national colors."

Limits were placed on Jews in every possible way. Here, an "Aryan" couple sits safely on a bench marked NOT FOR JEWS.

JEWS ARE NOT WANTED IN THIS TOWN. Signs like this appeared outside towns and villages everywhere.

Next, the Citizenship Law:

"A citizen of the Reich is only that subject of German or related blood who proves by his conduct that he is ready and able to serve the German people and the Reich faithfully."

"Only the full citizen of the Reich enjoys full political rights."

To remove any possibility of misunderstanding, clarifications made their appearance a few weeks later. "A Jew cannot be a citizen of the Reich. He has no right to vote in political affairs and he cannot hold public office."

A Jew was defined once and for all as a "person descended from at least three grandparents who are full Jews by race" and anyone who thought of himself as a Jew.

The Jews were now almost defenseless. They were completely outside the protection of the law. Signs saying JEWS NOT WANTED HERE or THE JEWS ARE OUR MISFORTUNE made their appearance outside cities and towns. Jews were forced out of towns and villages where their families had lived for generations so the town could declare itself *Judenrein*—"cleansed of Jews." Cafes and restaurants posted signs that said JEWS AND DOGS NOT PERMITTED HERE. Park benches were marked NOT FOR JEWS or FOR ARYANS ONLY. A Jewish doctor who gave his own blood to save a German's life was sentenced to seventeen months in a concentration camp for polluting the nation's blood or "defiling the race."

The 1936 Olympic Games were held in Berlin. The Nazis meant both the stadium and the games to demonstrate German superiority. Because of the large number of foreign visitors in the country, all visible anti-Semitic signs were removed and restrictions against Jews eased. Jesse Owens, called "the world's fastest man," won four gold medals. Rather than shake the hand of a black man, Hitler left the stadium.

GET OUT YOU FILTHY PIG! *Vicious cartoons and slogans made their appearance on Jewish shop and office windows.*

Property owned by Jews had to be registered with the government. This was the first step in a series that ended with Jewish businesses being "Aryanized"—sold cheaply or given to non-Jewish Germans.

If a Jew did not have a "recognizably Jewish" name, the women had to add "Sarah" and the men "Israel" as middle names to those they had. The government published a list of over one hundred "recognizably Jewish" names. It included Menachem, Isidor, Baruch, Ziporah, Chana, Beine.

All passports and identity cards belonging to Jews were stamped with a *J* or the word *Jude*.

Seventeen thousand Jews originally from Poland or of Polish nationality were expelled from Germany and dumped in a small town across the Polish border. Polish authorities refused to accept them at first, and the Germans would not take them back. They were forced to live for weeks in filthy, manure-covered stables until Poland changed its mind.

KRISTALLNACHT (CRYSTAL NIGHT)

The parents of seventeen-year-old Herschel Grynszpan, a student in Paris, were among the Jews trapped in that tiny Polish border town. In rage and grief, he shot and killed a minor official at the German embassy in Paris.

The Nazis used this as an excuse to launch a giant pogrom against Jews and Jewish property. It has come to be called *Kristallnacht*, the German for "Crystal Night," because of the huge amounts of broken glass from smashed Jewish storefronts and homes that littered the streets all over Germany. It took place on the night and morning of November 9 and 10, 1938.

The Nazis wanted the events to appear spontaneous, an "expression of the people's rage at the murderous acts of the Jews." But they planned the pogrom carefully. Before the event, orders went out to Gestapo offices and police stations all over the country:

"At very short notice actions against Jews, especially their synagogues, will take place throughout Germany. They are not to be hindered."

SS offices received this instruction: "Such measures are to be taken that do not entail danger to German life and property."

Kristallnacht, November 9, 1938. Jewish storefronts were smashed all over Germany. The stores were looted and destroyed.

Approximately one thousand synagogues were burned or destroyed during Kristallnacht.

An order sent to the city of Mannheim left little to the imagination:

"All the Jewish synagogues within the Fiftieth Brigade are to be blown up or set on fire immediately. Neighboring houses occupied by Aryans are not to be damaged." It concluded:

"This action is to be carried out in civilian clothes."

Ninety-one Jews were killed throughout the country. Suicides were common; the number is unknown. Over 30,000 Jewish males were sent to concentration camps—almost the entire male Jewish population between eighteen and sixty-five at the time. Approximately one thousand synagogues throughout Germany were burned or demolished, and over 7,500 businesses set on fire or otherwise destroyed. The Nazis' own figures admit to 815 shops, 29 department stores and 171 houses destroyed. They were certain, however, that "the true figures must be several times greater."

Goering, Goebbels and other high-ranking Nazis held a meeting about what to do next. The result: Jews were to make all needed repairs themselves and pay for them as well. Any insurance money they collected was to be turned over to the Reich. And they were fined one billion reichsmarks—then close to $500 million. They were to pay this, it was explained, to make up for their "terrible crime" against the German people. Said Goering, "I would not like to be a Jew in Germany now."

The front page of Der Stürmer (The Great Storm), an extremely popular anti-Semitic newspaper. Its owner and publisher, Julius Streicher, was a great favorite of Hitler. The issue here is devoted to the Blood Libel. It says that "Jews lust after the blood of non-Jews." This reaches a climax "at their Easter festival, Pesach [Passover]," when "they prefer to kill non-Jewish children." They "do this in a most horrible and gruesome manner . . . and collect the blood in a bowl. They drink the blood or use it for 'religious rites'." The line under the paper's title says, FIGHT FOR THE TRUTH. At the bottom, repeated every issue: THE JEWS ARE OUR MISFORTUNE.

The Nazis were not finished yet. Law after law against the Jews appeared. All their valuables had to be turned over to the Reich. Jews were not allowed to have radios, use telephones, have pets, buy flowers or go to barbers or beauty salons. They could not buy rationed food, go to school, use swimming pools.

In September 1941, "All Jews from the age of six are forbidden to appear in public without displaying the Jewish star." For the first time since the Middle Ages centuries earlier, a Jewish badge made its appearance in the civilized world as a mark of shame.

In October 1941 Jews were forbidden to leave their homes without permission. They could no longer leave their country. They were trapped.

Jews forced to scrub the streets while Hitler Youth and police stand by.

WHY DID THEY STAY?

There were over 500,000 Jews in Germany when Hitler came to power in 1933. By 1939 over 300,000 had left for other countries. In 1941 only 164,000 remained.

Why did they wait so long? Why did even that many stay? The reasons are many and complicated. The Nazis wanted them to leave. They wanted a Jew-free country. But as difficult as things were for the Jews, they were reluctant to go. They paid a heavy "security tax" if they left, signed all their property over to the government, and were allowed to take very little with them. Thus they would have to give up what they had spent their lives working for. They had to start over again with almost empty pockets in an unknown country, populated by people who were strangers to them.

And "starting over" is never an easy thing to do. To begin life again in a new country where they did not know the language and could not work at their original jobs or professions was very difficult. How would they live until they could speak the new language well? How could they earn their living? Leaving meant losing everything familiar and dear to them. Germany was their country; it was home.

The Nazis tricked Jews into a false security time after time. They would enact a law, put it into effect and then months would go by before any more government-approved violence would occur. German Jews knew their country to be extremely civilized, and it most certainly was. Some of the world's greatest musicians, philosophers and scientists came from there. They could not believe that things could get worse. Each time, they told themselves that it could not go on, that no more would happen. They could not imagine the worst that was to come. No one in the world could imagine that.

Jews had lived in Germany for almost two thousand years. They had made important contributions to the arts and sciences, to philosophy, business and finance, medicine and law. They had fought—and died—in Germany's wars. Perhaps more than Jews in any other country, they felt inseparably a part of their homeland. "More German than the Germans," it was said, and with pride.

Now they could no longer live their own lives. Soon they would not be allowed to live.

3

THE GHETTOS

Today I am going to play the prophet. If international
Jewry should succeed in . . . plunging Europe into a
world war, the result shall not be . . . a victory of
Judaism but the annihilation of the Jews of Europe.
—Adolf Hitler

WORLD WAR II BEGAN ON SEPTEMBER 1, 1939, when Germany invaded
Poland, and England and France came to its defense. Poland surrendered in
less than a month.

JEWS IN EASTERN EUROPE

Jews had been in Poland at least since the 1300s. Their style of life and their
distribution around the country were very different from that of the Jews of
Germany and the rest of Western Europe.

Outside of Poland and Eastern Europe, Jews lived almost entirely in
cities, made up a relatively small part of the population, and were more or
less integrated into their societies. They looked and behaved like everyone
else and spoke the same language.

To the east, however, especially in Poland, although the greater number
lived in the cities, the large remainder was scattered in thousands of small
towns and villages. Much more so than to the west, they lived in rural communities. Jews also made up a greater percentage of the population. In some
areas it was as high as 30 percent. Often they formed separate and easily
identifiable communities, in both cities and towns. Some villages were
entirely Jewish; cities and towns had their Jewish quarters.

These Jews were teachers, merchants, shoemakers, musicians, business-
men, mothers, fathers and children like any other people. Many were
extremely devout and spent much of their time in religious study. Religion

ABOVE: *German soldiers took great delight in cutting off the beards of religious Jews, sometimes with bayonets or even more painfully.*

LEFT: *Tormenting an old Jewish woman in Warsaw.*

shaped their lives, behavior and even determined the way they dressed. The most religious men wore hats and long coats, and had beards and sidelocks. Among themselves they spoke Yiddish, their Jewish language, not Polish; in the smaller towns many could not even speak Polish. When the Germans invaded Russia in 1941, they found the Jewish population there living in much the same way as the Polish Jews.

So in their language, customs and dress, they were set off from the populations around them. Their culture was rich, complex and vibrant with life. It has been said that these Eastern European Jews were the creative wellspring, the very heart and soul of all the Judaism in the world. The Nazis brought a stop to that life forever.

THE NAZIS IN EASTERN EUROPE

There were probably three major reasons why the Germans set up the ghettos, began the mass murders and later established most of the concentration camps and all of the death camps in Poland and Eastern Europe.

The rabbi in the cart is pulled by harnessed Jews instead of horses. The inscription on the back of the photograph reads, JEWS PUT TO WORK.

The Warsaw ghetto wall being built. Jews were taxed to pay the German firm that built it.

First, obviously, because nearly all of Europe's Jews were there—five million of them.

Second, the land area was vast. Aside from the major cities, many lightly populated forested miles separated communities from one another. By today's standards, communications among them were simple and primitive. All this allowed the Nazis some element of surprise. Their intended victims were less likely to resist if they did not know what was coming. It also permitted some secrecy. The Germans wanted to hide what they were doing from the attention of the rest of the world. In this they were not quite successful, as later chapters will show.

Third, Eastern Europe had a history of anti-Semitism, of which the Germans were well aware. There had been large-scale pogroms as recently as twenty years earlier. Individual anti-Semitic incidents occurred often. The Nazis planned to take as much advantage of this as they could.

JEWISH AREA—ENTRANCE FORBIDDEN. A gate to the Warsaw ghetto.

When Poland surrendered, the Germans made sections of the country part of Germany. Another large area, approximately in the center and to the south, was placed entirely under German control, particularly that of the SS. They gave Nazi-occupied Poland the name of *Generalgouvernement*—General Government.

Jewish businesses were "Aryanized." Jews were expelled from the schools, forbidden to enter parks, theaters and libraries and forced to wear the Yellow Star. All the anti-Jewish regulations put into effect in Germany were applied here, too. The Germans seemed to reserve a special viciousness for the Jews of Poland.

Looting, vandalism, acts of sadistic cruelty, torture and murder began almost immediately. Sometimes the acts were aimed at the religion—a rabbi was made to spit on the Torah, the sacred book of Jewish law, holy to all Jews. A group of Jews was forced to run a race through their synagogue on hands and knees, and each "winner" was shot as he came crawling out of the door. Jews were picked up off the streets and taken as forced labor to dig ditches or cut down trees, and sometimes were never seen again. German

soldiers cut off the beards of pious Jews with bayonets or pulled them out by the roots, even set them on fire. They performed "medical" examinations on women to find "hidden valuables." They used Jews for target practice.

Five thousand Jews were killed within the first two months of the Nazi takeover of Poland.

THE GHETTOS ARE ESTABLISHED

Reinhard Heydrich was the Chief of the Reich Security Main Office. On September 21, 1939, he issued a directive called "The Jewish Question in Occupied Territory." It ordered that all Jews in Nazi-occupied areas were to be moved to special places set aside for them in or near main cities—the ghettos.

Jews were expelled from their homes, from towns and villages where their families had lived for generations. Carrying pitiful odds and ends of their past lives with them, they were marched or shipped in freight cars to the ghettos. Many died on the way from hunger, thirst, exhaustion or murder.

The first ghetto was set up in the city of Lodz, Poland. The order establishing it made it clear that this was only one step toward the Nazis' final goal. The order came from SS Brigadier General Friedrich Uebelhoer:

"The creation of the ghetto is obviously only a temporary measure. When and by what means the ghetto, and the town of Lodz, will be cleansed of

Young and old begged in the streets.

Jews I reserve to myself. Our final objective must be, in any case, to burn out this plague boil completely."

The "final objective" was only in the early planning stages. For the time being, the ghettos would hold the Jews until the Nazis were ready to go on with the next stage.

Ghettos were located in the oldest, most run-down sections of town. The buildings were in bad condition, often near collapse. Where running water and sanitary facilities existed, the overcrowding soon made them break down.

The ghetto in Lodz was a little over 1.5 miles square—the size of about twenty city blocks. Over 150,000 Jews lived seven or eight to a room.

Children suffered the most from hunger and cold. Children "who are dying of hunger. They howl, beg, sing, moan, shiver with cold . . . without shoes, in rags, sacks . . . children swollen with hunger, disfigured, half-conscious. . . ."

Ghetto ration card for October 1941. This card officially entitled the holder to 300 calories daily.

In the Vilna, Lithuania, ghetto, 25,000 people lived in seventy-two buildings on five streets. The crowding was so intense that each person had about seven feet to call his or her own—a space "as narrow as the grave."

The Warsaw ghetto in Poland took up approximately 1.6 square miles. It held anywhere from 400,000 to 600,000 Jews during its existence—the lower number almost the population of the entire state of Wyoming. Eight to ten people lived in each room; that figure went up to fourteen when the area of the ghetto was reduced.

Most of the ghettos were enclosed. Some were surrounded by fences or barbed wire, as in Lodz, or by a wall, as in Warsaw—which the Jews had to pay a German firm to build. The ghetto wall in Cracow, Poland, was made of gravestones from the Jewish cemetery.

Jews were forbidden to leave the ghetto without a special permit, under penalty of death. Non-Jews without passes were not permitted to enter. The penalty might be carried out by shooting on the spot.

The supervision and final control of the ghettos lay with the Nazis. But at their order, twelve leading men were chosen from each ghetto to form a

Jewish Council. These men were made responsible for the day-to-day running of the ghetto. They were in charge of health, housing and public order. The councils ran hospitals, opened soup kitchens and distributed the food. In the large ghettos they even set up a Jewish police force. They were, in other words, the government of those captured cities within cities. The Jewish Councils were also responsible for carrying out any and all Nazi orders at every step of the ghettos' existence.

Jews in the ghetto worked whenever they could. They repaired old uniforms and clothes, produced such things as wooden and leather shoes, mattresses, ammunition boxes, baskets and brooms. Their best customers were the Germans, particularly the army. They also produced most of what helped keep the ghetto functioning.

German-owned and SS businesses functioned both inside and outside the larger ghettos; most were in Warsaw. The businesses took their workforce from the ghetto population. To have such a job meant a backbreaking ten- or twelve-hour day. The work permit that came with it entitled the laborer to a very small extra bit of money and a slightly larger food ration.

STARVATION

Starvation was deliberate Nazi policy. The amount of food the ghetto was allowed could change from week to week, sometimes from day to day. But the official weekly ration for the Jews in the General Government—described as "a populace that does no work worth mentioning"—was very small. At its very best, it was no more than 1,100 calories a day. But there were long periods when not even that much food was made available. For one week that was not unusual, these were the amounts each Jew was allowed:

Bread	14.0 oz.
Meat products	4.5 oz.
Sugar	1.75 oz.
Fat	.9 oz.

At its worst, that meant the Jewish ration was only about 350 calories a day, sometimes as little as 220 calories. An adult who sits at a desk for eight hours a day needs about 2,000 calories to keep his weight. A thirteen-year-old boy needs about 3,000, and a baby needs 1,200. With much less than those amounts, the body loses weight quickly. After a certain point, it begins to feed on itself, and muscle disappears. The body melts away. Painful death from starvation comes not long after that.

Starvation was the Jews' greatest torture. It was endless and could not be escaped. It shaped the lives of all who lived within the ghetto walls. From an inhabitant, here is a description of the conditions it created:

"Starvation was the lament of the beggars sitting in the street with their homeless families. Starvation was the cry of the mothers whose newborn babies wasted away and died. Men fought tooth and nail over a raw potato. Children risked their lives smuggling in a handful of turnips, for which whole families were waiting."

When the begging failed, people died in the street. "In the early morning, the corpses of beggars, children, old people, young people and women are lying in every street—the victims of the hunger and the cold. . . . " A woman seen begging in the morning would be found dead in the same spot in the evening. Passersby covered the bodies with newspapers until the hearse—a flat wooden cart—could come and remove them.

The elderly and the sick suffered the most and died the soonest. And the children, "the countless children, whose parents had perished, sitting in the

"The entire population seemed to be living in the streets." The overcrowding of eight, ten or more to a room brought them outside to join the homeless already there.

streets. Their bodies are frightfully thin, the bones stick out of a yellow skin that looks like parchment. . . . They crawl on all fours, groaning. . . . ”

In 1940, the first year of the Warsaw ghetto, 90 people died of starvation. In 1941 the figure rose to 11,000. At its height, starvation killed 500 each week.

Let the Nazis' own figures tell the story. Here is the Warsaw ghetto death rate from all causes for the first eight months of 1941, as reported by Heinz Auerswald, Nazi commissioner for the area:

January	898
February	1,023
March	1,608
April	2,061
May	3,821
June	4,290
July	5,550
August	5,560

Children made the best smugglers. Here, one returns safely through the wall.

THE COLD

Poland's winters are cold—bitter cold. January temperatures in Warsaw can drop to less than 20 degrees below zero. If the Nazis would not allow Jews food, they surely would not allow them fuel. They even took away the warmest clothes. All sheepskin and furs, even fur-lined gloves, had to be turned in for the use of the soldiers at the front or civilians back home in Germany.

There was not enough kerosene, coal—"black pearls"—or wood. Anything that would burn was used for a moment's heat. Apartments were taken apart. Old buildings were dismantled. Mobs swarmed over them, taking them down piece by piece, knocking apart walls that sometimes collapsed and injured or killed.

Wrapped in rags, bundled in pieces of worn clothing too big or too small, they huddled in the streets—the children. "The most fearful sight is that of freezing children, dumbly weeping in the street, with bare feet, bare knees, and torn clothing."

A child wrote in her diary, "I am hungry. I am cold. When I grow up I want to be a German, and then I will no longer be hungry or cold."

DISEASE

Weakened by starvation, ghetto inhabitants made easy victims for disease. The great number of people crammed into an area intended for only a fraction of that amount overwhelmed what limited sanitary facilities there were. Sewage pipes froze in winter and burst. Human waste was put in the streets with the garbage, and the starving homeless had to use the streets themselves as toilets. Little water was available, and soap was a luxury few could find or afford.

People who died of so-called natural causes—heart disease, cancer, pneumonia—died sooner and in greater numbers because of the lack of sufficient food, drugs and decent dwellings. But typhus, a disease directly connected with overcrowding and filth, took by far the greatest number.

During 1941 in the Warsaw ghetto, almost 16,000 people died of typhus. That is the official number. But the Jewish Council had good reason not always to report the true number. Typhus is highly contagious, and the

Nazis were afraid of epidemics. Soldiers would come unannounced into the ghetto and remove those sick with typhus, and they would never be seen again. The Jewish Council lied so that at least some of the sick would have time to get well again. The correct number of those who died of typhus in that one year is thought to be closer to 100,000.

The Streets

Jews from all over Eastern Europe were brought to the biggest ghettos, which would have made them crowded enough. The next stage of the Nazi plan brought Jews from all over the continent—from Austria, Holland, Germany, France, Greece—from all the countries under German control. They were being held in the ghettos, although they did not know it, until the Nazi "Final Solution" could be brought into action.

The terrible overcrowding, with seven to ten or more in each room, brought inhabitants outside in the daylight hours. There they joined the homeless in aimlessly walking through the streets.

A non-Jewish Pole brought to the Warsaw ghetto for a brief visit described what he saw:

"These were still living people, if you could call them such. For apart from their skin, eyes, and voice there was nothing human left in these palpitating figures. Everywhere there was hunger, misery, the atrocious stench of decomposing bodies, the pitiful moans of dying children, the desperate cries and gasps of a people struggling for life against impossible odds. . . .

"The entire population seemed to be living in the streets. There was hardly a square yard of empty space. As we picked our way across the mud and rubble, the shadows of what had once been men or women flitted by us in pursuit of someone or something, their eyes blazing with some insane hunger or greed."

Smuggling

If the ghetto can be said to have a life's blood, then the smugglers kept it flowing. It is even possible that if it had not been for the smugglers, the Nazis would have succeeded in starving the ghettos to death.

Soup for starving orphans, supplied by the Jewish Council whenever possible.

There was some large-scale smuggling, but most of it day by day was small. Workers outside smuggled in whatever they could. Those who could afford it bribed guards not to notice.

If the Jews were caught smuggling anything—no matter how small—the penalty was death, sometimes by being shot immediately. Here is the official report of a German guard in the Lodz ghetto:

"On December 1, 1941, I was on duty between 2:00 and 4:00 P.M. at Sentry Point No. 4 in Holstein Street. At 3:00 P.M. I saw a Jewess climb onto the fence of the ghetto, stick her hand through the fence, and try to steal some turnips from a passing cart. I made use of my firearm. The Jewess received two fatal shots.

"Type of firearm: carbine 98

"Ammunition used: 2 cartridges

"[signed] Sergeant Naumann"

Some were not so lucky as to be killed right away. A Jewish mother was caught buying an egg from a Polish peasant. Both were held until ghetto inhabitants could be gathered to watch. Then they were hanged. Their bodies were not removed for three days "as a lesson to all who would learn."

Most of the smugglers were children ten to fourteen years old. Their small, thin bodies could slip under a hole in the barbed wire or through a chink in the wall and get back the same way. If they were successful, then starvation was postponed for another day. If they were not, they might be shot as their waiting mothers watched. Sometimes they too were not lucky enough to suffer the penalty right away. An adult remembered:

"Once when I was walking along the wall, I came across a 'smuggling operation' being carried out by children. The actual operation seemed to be over. There was only one thing left to do. The little Jewish boy on the other side of the wall had to slip back inside the ghetto through his hole, bringing with him the last piece of booty. Half the little boy was already visible when he began to cry out.

"At the same time, loud abuse in German could be heard from the Aryan side. I hurried to help the child, meaning to pull him quickly through the hole. Unhappily, the boy's hips stuck fast in the gap in the wall. Using both hands, I tried with all my might to pull him through. He continued to scream dreadfully. I could hear the police on the other side beating him savagely. . . .

"When I finally succeeded in pulling the boy through the hole, he was already dying. His backbone was crushed."

JEWISH LIFE

The ghetto was a giant cage, its thousands of imprisoned inhabitants forced there from all walks of life, from all occupations, skills and abilities.

In the midst of the vast Nazi terror, suffering from starvation and disease, and with death all around them, these doomed people gave the ghetto some of the variety and vitality of a true city.

Polish and Yiddish posters announced cultural and social events in the ghetto.

Teaching was forbidden, yet there were secret classes in history, languages, the arts—with examinations, grades and even diplomas.

Theatrical groups, professional and amateur, put on plays.

Noted authorities and scholars gave lectures.

Musicians gave concerts, singers put on recitals.

Scientists conducted experiments.

Operas were composed and performed.

Secret libraries sprang up, with long waiting lists for books—history, political science, cheap novels, classics, poetry, romances, adventure stories.

How very alive they were, these Jews, in the face of the Nazi desire for their deaths.

THE END OF THE GHETTOS

It has been estimated that one-fifth of ghetto inhabitants died of disease and hunger-related illnesses. At that rate, the entire population of all the ghettos would have died out within five or six years. But that was not fast enough.

Chief of Security Reinhard Heydrich explained: "The evacuation of the Jews to the East . . . provide[s] practical experience of great importance, in view of the coming Final Solution of the Jewish Question."

4

SPECIAL ACTION GROUPS AND THEIR HELPERS

I can state with pride that my men . . . are proud to
act out of conviction and fidelity to their Führer.
—Eduard Strauch, Special Action Group A

This is a glorious page in our history that has never
been written and never shall be written.
—Heinrich Himmler, Supreme Leader of the SS

SPECIAL ACTION GROUPS

THEY CAME, WITHIN TWO OR THREE DAYS of the army as it advanced through Russia. In small groups they combed the areas, coming back in days or weeks if they had not completed their task.

They were the *Einsatzgruppen*—the Special Action Groups. They were mobile firing squads made up of men specially trained for their task. The procedure was carefully worked out. After the war, one of their leaders described it this way:

The assigned unit "would enter a village or a city and order the prominent Jewish citizens to call together all Jews for the purpose of resettlement. They were requested to hand over their valuables to the leaders of the unit, and shortly before the execution to surrender their outer clothing. The men, women and children were led to a place of execution, which in most cases was located next to a more deeply excavated antitank ditch. Then they were shot, kneeling or standing, and the corpses thrown into the ditch."

A secret report from Jews in Warsaw gave a few more details:

"Men from fourteen to sixty were rounded up in one place—a square or a cemetery—where they were slaughtered, machine-gunned or killed by hand grenades. They had to dig their own graves. Children in orphanages,

A detachment of Special Action Group D on its arrival at a small town in Poland.

inmates of old-age homes, and the hospitalized sick were shot, women were killed in the streets. In many towns Jews were taken away to an unknown destination and executed in nearby woods."

The report of SS Colonel Jäger, leader of Special Action Group 3, described one of his assignments:

"The Jews had to be collected in one or more towns and a ditch had to be dug at the right site for the right number. The marching distance from collecting points to the ditches averaged three miles. The Jews were brought in groups of 500, separated by at least 1.2 miles, to the place of execution. . . . In Roskiskis 3,208 people had to be transported three miles before they could be liquidated. . . .

"Only careful planning enabled the men to carry out five actions a week. . . . "

Mobile killing vans were put into use. These trucks were specially designed to pipe exhaust fumes from the engine into the back of the van. The Jews sealed inside did not live very long. The purpose of these gray trucks came to be known and people ran away when they drove into the towns. The men of the firing squads continued to do the job personally. A participant described his work:

"The execution itself lasted three–four hours. I took part in the execution the whole time. The only pauses I made were when my carbine was empty and I had to reload. It is therefore not possible for me to say how

Jews forced to dig their own graves.

Members of a Special Action Group at work.

many Jews I myself killed in these three–four hours as during this time someone else shot in my place. During these times we drank quite a lot of schnapps to stimulate our zeal for our work."

THE ORDER POLICE

These were ordinary men. They were not specially trained for their task. Most were not even members of the Nazi party. They were policemen, wearing green uniforms instead of the field gray of the soldier or SS man.

The policemen of the Third Reich performed many of the same tasks as police everywhere. But these, called the *Ordnungspolizei*—the Order Police—were given another task. They did their work along with the Special Action Groups in Poland and in Russia. In some cases, they joined the Special Action Groups; in others, they acted on their own.

They rounded up Jews, shot Jews too weak or too slow, guarded Jews in their collecting places in various towns and ghettos, marched them to the killing sites, and there they killed Jews in the same manner as the Special Action Groups.

These policemen were given one assignment somewhat different from the Special Action Groups. They were told that their special task, aside from

VON DER EINSATZGRUPPE A DURCHGEFÜHRTE JUDENEXEKUTIONEN

Report to SS chief Heinrich Himmler from Special Action Group A. The four countries are Estonia, Latvia, Lithuania and Belorussia, all part of the Soviet Union. Figures by the caskets are the number of Jews killed, other figures the number remaining alive. Estonia is "free of Jews" after 963 were killed.

aiding in the mass murders, was to capture Jews who had managed to escape the roundups. They called it "The Jew Hunt." They spent hours combing the surrounding countryside and shot any hiding Jew they found. Said one, "I must admit that we felt a certain joy when we would seize a Jew one of us could kill."

The Order Police were aided by auxiliary police forces recruited from among Estonians, Ukrainians, Latvians and others from Eastern Europe. Under the directions of the Order Police, these units performed the same deeds. At times the only Germans present at the execution sites were the officers in charge.

Although not all were among the killers, the Order Police played a major role in the extermination of the Jews. Said Himmler to his SS: "The actions of the man in the green jacket [of the police] are as important as your own." The full extent of their participation has only recently begun to be known.

It is estimated that two million Jews were killed in this way by the Special Action Groups and the Order Police.

THE REGULAR ARMY

Most Germans, even most of the world, believed that the regular German army—the *Wehrmacht*—was free of the murderous activities of the SS, Order Police and others. The men of the army have been considered dutiful soldiers, nothing more.

In 1995 a research group in Germany organized an exhibit called "The German Army and Genocide." The last word—*genocide*—means the deliberate and systematic destruction of an entire people who belong to one racial, political, cultural or religious group; here, the Jews. The exhibit was a collection of over one hundred photos, letters and other materials about the activities of the army on the eastern front and elsewhere outside of Western Europe.

The research that led to the exhibit uncovered evidence that army troops carried out murder operations. In addition, during the exhibit's tour of thirty-four German cities, men and women came forward and revealed their memories of mass murder. They brought soldiers' wartime letters and notebooks about the massacres, as well as photographs taken at various sites.

The men of the regular army acted on their own, sometimes voluntarily, as well as in cooperation with the Special

A mother with her two children sitting among a group of Jews assembled for mass execution.

A member of the German Order Police and a Ukrainian militiaman doing their job.

Action Groups. The latter depended on the army for food, fuel and ammunition; from commanding officer on down, the soldiers knew about the "special actions" against Jews. The commander of the Special Action Group operating in Ukraine reported, "From the first day onward, [the group] has succeeded in establishing an excellent understanding with all sections of the [army]."

A soldier identified only as Franz wrote to his parents on July 7, 1941, "So far we have sent about 1,000 Jews to the hereafter. But that's still too few." Still another wrote, "In Russia, wherever there is a German soldier, the Jews are no more."

On October 4, 1941, army General Franz Boehme asked for 2,100 prisoners from two concentration camps. They were to be shot in "atonement" for the death of twenty-one German soldiers. He went on:

"The shooting squads are to be drawn from the 342nd Division . . . and from the 449th Signal Corps Battalion. . . . "

First Lieutenant and Company Commander Liepe obeyed the order. In fact, he collected one hundred more Jews than required. His follow-up report was filed on October 13. Each section was carefully numbered. The following are some excerpts:

"1. *Order*

"Order was given to shoot 2,200 Jews from the camp in Belgrade . . . "

"4. *Transportation and Vehicles*

" . . . transportation of the soldiers involved was by army vehicles."

"7. *Film and Photography*

"Information & Press Company 'S.'"

"9. *Implementation*

"The prisoners were picked up . . . at 5:30 A.M. . . . The transport occurred with no difficulties.

" . . . The shootings were carried out using rifles at a distance of 12 meters [7.5 feet]. Five riflemen were ordered to shoot each prisoner. . . . Valuables and superfluous items were gathered and later delivered to the National Socialist Welfare or to the Security Police.

"The shooting was concluded at 6:30 P.M. There were no unusual occurrences. The units returned to their quarters satisfied. . . . "

There is no longer any doubt that the regular German army played an active role in the murder of civilians in Eastern Europe and in the killings of the Holocaust.

LOCAL HELPERS

By late 1941 over 40,000 Europeans had volunteered to fight alongside the Germans against the Russians. Though their exact numbers are not known, they played an important part in the murder of Europe's Jews.

In several Eastern European towns, the local population itself participated, "as they did in Kovno, Lithuania, where [prisoners] released from jail clubbed Jews to death with crowbars in plain sight of cheering crowds, with mothers holding up their children to enjoy the spectacle and soldiers milling around to watch the fun like a football match."

NAZI MENTAL HEALTH

Himmler had said, "All Jews that we can reach now during the war are to be exterminated without exception."

But the Nazis were not satisfied with the development of their plans so far. First, the killings were going too slowly. Second, the mass murders were effective, but they used ammunition needed at the front. The third reason was the most important of all. Auschwitz commander Rudolf Hoess reported Himmler's words:

"[It would be] impossible by shooting to dispose of the large number of people expected, [since] it would place too heavy a burden on the . . . men who had to carry it out, especially because of the women and children among its victims."

In other words, mass murder was too hard on the murderers.

The Nazis developed other plans for the Jews who remained.

A successful "Jew hunt."

5

THE FINAL SOLUTION

We cannot shoot these . . . Jews, we cannot poison
them. We shall, however, take measures that shall lead
to their eventual annihilation.

—Hans Frank,
Governor of Nazi-occupied Poland

NAZI GERMANY WAS AT THE PEAK OF ITS POWER IN 1941. The invasion of
Russia on June 22 had so far succeeded with lightning speed. Germany now
occupied or dominated almost all of Europe, east and west. The maps on
pages 54 and 55 show how much of the continent had come under its control in less than three years.

In all of Eastern Europe, Jews had been herded into ghettos. Jews elsewhere were gradually being isolated from their countrymen by the usual Nazi
regulations; some already were allowed to live only in certain restricted areas.

What were the Nazis to do with all those Jews? They were dying in the
ghettos, but that took too much time. The Special Action Groups and Order
Police were doing their work, but that was slow and inefficient. Their purpose was known now, and the Nazis were concerned that their intended victims would get away.

The mass killings in the east of Europe were not possible in smaller or
more populated countries to the west, such as Belgium, Holland and France.
There the people were concentrated in cities; the mobile firing squads did
not have large empty areas in which to hide evidence of their work. Also,
anti-Semitism was not as strong there as in Eastern Europe, and the non-
Jewish populations might try to help their country's Jews and become more
difficult to control. At the same time, these countries were closer to the
parts of the world not under Nazi control and in greater contact with them,
and the Germans did not want word of their actions to spread.

So the question of what to do with the Jews remained. The Germans
had tried forcing emigration to make their country and Austria free of Jews.

EUROPE BEFORE THE NAZIS, 1930

NAZI-DOMINATED EUROPE

They had even toyed with the idea of establishing a "Jewish homeland" on the French island of Madagascar off the coast of southeast Africa. Early plans had been drawn up for a self-sufficient colony of Jews there, all working under Nazi guard for the benefit of the Third Reich. Sterilization had been discussed as one way to make sure the "Jewish race" would die out.

But all such plans and ideas were dropped. With the takeover of Poland and the invasion of Russia, there were too many Jews for emigration to be practical. By their own count, including countries they had not yet fought or defeated, the Nazis estimated that they would eventually have eleven million Jews to deal with. There was no place large enough to hold them.

Concentration camps already existed in Germany and in almost all countries under German control. Both Jews and non-Jews were sent there. The guards were trained to be sadistic and conditions were inhuman. Many thousands had already died. But neither the camps nor the ghettos or the mass shootings were the answer to the Nazis' "Jewish Question." Other arrangements had to be made.

In the Auschwitz concentration camp in the summer of 1941, 250 hospital patients and 600 Russian prisoners of war were forced into a sealed room and killed with a poison gas called Zyklon B. The experiment, showing that it was possible to kill large groups at one time, was "a success"; construction of the death center at Auschwitz began, and was completed the following year.

At the Chelmno camp on December 8, 1941, the gassing vans used by the Special Action Groups were brought into use again. The mass killing of Jews with carbon monoxide fumes began on a daily basis.

The plans for the Final Solution of the Jewish Question had been set in motion.

THE CONFERENCE ON THE FINAL SOLUTION

"I herewith order you to make all necessary preparations . . . required for the complete solution of the Jewish question in European territories under German influence. . . .

"I further order you to submit to me as soon as possible an overall plan showing the measures for organization and action necessary to carry out the desired Final Solution of the Jewish Question."

Reinhard Heydrich, main architect of the Final Solution. Hitler called him "the Man with the Iron Heart."

Reinhard Heydrich, chief of Reich security, received this order from Field Marshall Hermann Goering on July 30, 1941. For reasons not yet known, there was nearly a five-month delay. But at last Heydrich called a conference to meet on January 20, 1942.

Senior officials from several departments and SS officers responsible for administering areas under German control gathered in an elegant house in Wannsee, a wealthy suburb of Berlin. Adolf Eichmann, head of Bureau IVB-4 in the Jewish Affairs Department, took notes.

Official copies of the notes quote the men using such colorless words as "solutions," "resettlements," "questions," "problems." Later, on trial for his life in Israel, Eichmann told the truth:

"These gentlemen . . . were discussing the subject quite bluntly from the language I had to use later in the record. During the conversation they

A mobile gassing van at Chelmno.

minced no words about it all . . . They spoke about methods of killing, about liquidation, about extermination."

It is almost impossible to imagine this. These men, most of them fairly well educated, all of them holding high rank and positions of importance, sat and discussed the best ways and means of murdering masses of people. They had lunch, they smoked, they were waited on by white-jacketed servants. No doubt they joked with one another, too, as people do at meetings. Eichmann remembered that "after this Wannsee conference we were sitting together peacefully, and not in order to talk shop, but in order to relax after the long hours of strain." They had worked out an efficient and careful plan that would mean the death of millions before it had run its course.

It was decided that Jews in the rest of Europe would be transported eastward to the ghettos in Nazi-occupied Poland and Russia. Starting with the Jews of the General Government, those declared fit for work would be deported to camps already built or being built to receive them. There they would be worked to death. Any who managed to survive would have shown themselves to be made of stronger stuff than the rest, and would be killed. Here is how Heydrich put it:

"Within the framework of the Final Solution, the Jews must be transferred to the East under appropriate guard, and there be assigned to the appropriate work service. Able-bodied Jews, separated by sex, will be brought in work gangs to those territories to build roads. It goes without saying that a large part of them will be eliminated by natural reduction.

"The remainder will have to be treated appropriately. This remainder represents a natural selection that, if freed, must be viewed as capable of forming the nucleus of a redeveloped Jewry."

The plan was the height of Nazi efficiency. Jewish labor would help Germany win the war, hundreds of thousands dying in the process and saving the Nazis the trouble of killing them. Then, when the war was won, those few remaining alive would be disposed of both because they were a danger and because they were no longer needed.

As it turned out, this plan was not followed exactly. Some Jews were kept alive for work. But millions were taken from the ghettos and immediately deported to their deaths.

Most of the plan remained unchanged, however. Transportation was arranged. A system was set up to find "able-bodied Jews" and to select the "unfit"—which meant children under twelve, the elderly, the sick and pregnant women. The Nazis made careful plans to take care of everything.

REINHARD HEYDRICH

Reinhard Heydrich had been thrown out of the German navy for "conduct unbecoming to an officer and a gentleman." He joined the Nazi party and the SS, and gradually worked his way up through the ranks to become a lieutenant general and the man in charge of security for the Third Reich. He was a tall, slim, blond man, with piercing, deep-set blue eyes. He deserved his nickname of the "Blond Beast."

Heydrich had shown himself to be absolutely without pity toward all judged "enemies of the state." His Gestapo and security police were feared everywhere, even among Germans. Heinrich Himmler, his superior and chief of the SS, gave him complete authority to carry out Hitler's order for the Final Solution. Hitler himself had called Heydrich "the Man with the Iron Heart."

Heydrich's car was bombed in Prague by members of the Czech resistance on May 27, 1942, and he died shortly thereafter.

The small mining town of Lidice in Czechoslovakia was chosen as the target of Nazi revenge. All the men and boys were shot, the women and children sent to concentration camps and the entire town razed to the ground. Its name was removed from German maps.

In honor of Heydrich, the extermination of the Jews of Poland was given the name of Operation Reinhard.

6

OTHER VICTIMS

The law of existence requires uninterrupted killing, so
that the better may live.

—Adolf Hitler

IN ONE WAY THE NAZIS WERE POSITIVELY DEMOCRATIC. Any group they found
inferior to themselves was treated with the greatest brutality. Even within
their own country they found groups to rout out, all for the betterment of
"fatherland, folk, and Führer."

Only Jews were to be wiped from the face of the earth. But five other
groups were also marked for what the Nazis called "special treatment." The
five were the incurably sick, Gypsies, homosexual men, the Polish leading
classes and Russian prisoners of war.

THE INCURABLY SICK

Hitler signed an order on September 1, 1939, that called for the start of
Operation T4. Doctors were allowed to select the incurably sick so that they
could be killed. The order described them as "life unworthy of life." The
"mercy killing," or euthanasia, was carried out on the following:

- The senile
- The mentally retarded, adults and children
- All Jews in mental hospitals
- Individuals who had been treated in any hospital, asylum, nursing home
  and so on for at least five years
- Deformed newborn babies
- Epileptics
- Invalids unable to work
- Victims of incurable disease that made them unable to work

For the purity of Aryan blood, these sick people had to die. Keeping them alive was also uneconomical, because they produced nothing and were examples, the Nazis said, of the "useless eaters" in the nation.

At first some were starved to death, especially children; others were given lethal poisonous injections. But this was inefficient. Two years before their use by the Special Action Groups in Eastern Europe, mobile killing vans made their appearance. Operation T4 marked the first use of gas chambers during the Third Reich as well, nearly eighteen months before the "successful experiment" in Auschwitz involving large groups. Exhaust fumes were piped inside sealed rooms, either from a truck's engine or from tanks

The graveyard at the Hadamar Institute, a major site for Operation T4, the killing of German "lives unworthy of life."

of carbon monoxide. At special centers set up for the purpose, small groups were gassed to death.

The two SS men in charge of this operation—Christian Wirth and Victor Brack—used the experience gained here when it was time for the mass murder of Jews in 1941.

After the patient was dead, a letter went to his or her family saying that their relative had died of "heart failure," and "considering his grave illness, life for the deceased meant torture. Thus you must look upon his death as a release." The bodies were cremated.

But the German people had come to understand what was happening. Hundreds of letters of protest were written and condemnation came loudly from the churches. On Hitler's order the program was stopped in 1941.

Operation T4 had killed over 100,000 "unworthy lives," including more than 3,000 children, by that time. Although officially stopped, it continued secretly throughout the war and even beyond. A severely disabled four-year-old boy was murdered on May 29, 1945—weeks after Germany surrendered. Some participants in T4 believed that the program would have begun again fully if Germany had won the war, this time including the civilians and soldiers made invalids by the war Germany had started.

THE GYPSIES (ROMANIES)

Two major groups of Gypsies, the Roma and Sinti, had been in Germany since the fifteenth century. That made them citizens under Nazi law. Not comfortable with that, Nazi lawyers broke all German Gypsies into two categories, "sedentary" and "nomadic." The first were those who had settled down in homes and held steady jobs; most of them were permitted to remain unharmed where they were. The second were Gypsies who wandered from place to place in the traditional Gypsy way; they were imprisoned in concentration camps as "asocials," a Nazi-invented category of people unfit for civilized society.

Official policy called their presence "the Gypsy menace." Himmler himself had said that Gypsies "should be removed from Europe as a race of little value." They were believed to weaken any society or country by their presence alone. Before long, they faced restrictions similar to those placed on the Jews, although they did not have to wear identifying marks or badges on their clothes. They were settled in ghettolike camps or areas within Jewish ghettos. Thousands were sent to concentration or death camps, especially Auschwitz, where all were gassed; the Special Action Groups took their toll among Gypsies, too.

Because they are a nomadic people and live primarily on the fringes of society, facts and figures are hard to come by. Based on population figures in all the countries involved from before and after the war, estimates range from 300,000 to over one million Gypsies killed by the Nazis. The Gypsies call this period in their history "The Devouring."

HOMOSEXUALS—GAY MEN

Himmler said it plainly: Homosexuality is "a symptom of degeneracy that could destroy our race—we must return to the guiding [ancient] principle: extermination of degenerates."

The Nazis wanted an increased German birthrate, so homosexuals were useless to the nation—as long as they remained homosexual. Nazi attempts at "rehabilitation" involved such things as transplantation of male hormones and forced time with prostitutes. An unknown number was sterilized or castrated. Existing Nazi records show that these attempts were not successful in "converting" homosexuals into heterosexuals.

Homosexuality had been punishable by German law since 1871. Under the Nazis, any German civilian male convicted of homosexuality would serve out his jail time and then be sent to a concentration camp; most were sent directly there without trial or jail. Wearing the pink cloth triangle that marked him as homosexual, he was permitted to live and work only with other homosexuals.

The cruelties and brutalities were as harsh as for other concentration camp inmates. They were worse in only one way: other prisoners mistreated them as well. Torture and beatings were usually aimed at the genitals.

Homosexuals in Germany, as elsewhere in the world at that time, formed a hidden society, and Nazi records are not complete. Estimates of victims range from around 20,000 to 500,000 male homosexuals killed.

There were no laws against lesbianism. First, because women were considered much less important than men. Second, because no German woman could possibly reject the attentions of a healthy "Aryan" male. Third, because the Nazis could not imagine that a German woman would not want to bear children for the sake of the Reich.

THE POLISH LEADING CLASSES

The Nazis believed that some people were beneath the true human level. They called them *Untermenschen*—subhumans. The Jews, considered a menace and threat to the whole human race, had to be destroyed completely. The subhumans would be allowed to live, but only without any power of their own and only as slave labor for Germany.

All Eastern Europeans were included, especially the Slavs—Poles, Ukrainians and Russians—and also Latvians, Estonians, Lithuanians and others. The Nazis planned to move them out of large areas and move in Germans, either from Germany itself or ethnic Germans, those born outside the country but raised as Germans.

Probably because Poland had the largest single population and greatest land area entirely under their control, the Nazis began the operation there; Russia and the other countries would follow when Germany won the war.

If the people were to be a moldable mass under German domination, doing only as their conquerors wanted, it was necessary to begin by removing all leaders living among them. That meant the creative and educated—artists and writers, officers in the armed forces, doctors, lawyers, priests, teachers and so on. They were rounded up and sent to concentration camps. Most died of camp conditions or were shot.

The Nazis had plans to go on from there. Future generations would be prevented from rising above the subhuman level, at least as Poles. "If necessary," said Himmler, "by taking away their children and bringing them up with us." The Germans had even given thought to Polish schools. As described by Himmler, they would include only "simple arithmetic up to 500; writing one's own name; the lesson that it is a divine commandment to be obedient to the Germans; and to be honest, hardworking and good. I do not think reading is required."

The Nazis lost the war before they could bring their full plan into effect. What they did manage to carry out was terrible enough.

Heinrich Himmler, chief of the SS. Responsible only to Hitler, his power was almost unlimited.

Of the three million non-Jewish Poles killed during World War II, over one million were the most educated and creative people in the nation.

SOVIET PRISONERS OF WAR

The people of the Soviet Union were slated for "special treatment" for two reasons. First, they were Eastern European Slavs and therefore subhumans. Second, they came from a communist nation, and communism was almost a synonym for Judaism to the Nazis.

The Germans had not yet conquered the country, but prisoner-of-war camps made an easy place for them to start carrying out their plans. Not only were the captured soldiers Russian; they had also actively fought against the Nazis. They therefore required especially harsh treatment.

In May 1944 the German army estimated that it had captured 5.16 million Russian prisoners of war, most in the first campaigns of 1941. Only 1,871,000 were still alive; 473,000 were listed as "executed" and 67,000 had escaped. The arithmetic yields about 3 million dead.

Most Soviet prisoners of war were kept in large cages, open pens with no shelter, surrounded by fences or barbed wire. They died of exposure or starved to death. When they did not die in the so-called camps, they were used for medical experiments or as guinea pigs in the first gas chambers built in the killing centers.

That is how the Nazi "bringers of civilization" treated the "inferior peoples" in the parts of the world held under their control.

7

DEPORTATIONS

Not much will be left of the Jews. . . . The prophecy
the Führer made about them is beginning to come
true in a most terrible manner.

—Joseph Goebbels

ROUNDUPS

"ON AUGUST 11, 1942, THE SS, SD, and the mounted police fell like a pack
of savages on the Zamosc Jewish quarter. It was a complete surprise. The
brutes on horseback, particularly, created a panic; they raced through the
streets shouting insults, slashing about on all sides with their whips. Our
community then numbered about 10,000 people. In a twinkling, without
their even realizing what happened, about 3,000 men, women, and children, picked up haphazardly in the streets and in the houses, were driven to
the station to be deported to an unknown destination."

So began the deportation to the camps from the Polish ghetto of
Zamosc.

But the shock and confusion of that roundup was not the Germans' preferred approach. They wanted the collection of Jews for deportation to go
smoothly, with as little disorder as possible. Indeed, best of all would be if
the Jews reported voluntarily. To get them to do so, the Germans used all
kinds of lies and tricks to mislead them.

Most often the Germans called the deportations "resettlement in the
East." They claimed conditions would be better. There would be work for
the willing and the fit, more food, improved housing and doctors to care for
the sick. In some parts of Greece, Jews were told they could exchange their
Greek money for Polish money to convince them that "resettlement in the
East" was the truth. Jews in parts of Poland were told that work awaited
them in Germany, and their Polish money was exchanged for German
reichsmarks. In one ghetto, those who reported on their own were given

Her last moments at home. In a few hours she was deported with her family to a camp. She survived the war and is living in the United States.

A mother with her babies at the moment of deportation.

warm clothes for the journey. Most cruel of all, the Nazis promised an extra ration of food. The starving Jews reported, were given their bread, ate it ravenously, and then were herded into freight cars and shipped to their deaths.

The lies and deceptions took on endless variations. For example, fifteen hundred Jews were needed for work "in a fish factory"; nineteen hundred reported voluntarily. Several hundred "educated and young" Jews were needed for "record-keeping work"; thousands came.

The lie about work was easy to believe. It made sense that a country at war needed all the workers it could find. It did not make sense to destroy a labor force of such size. The fact that the Nazis did just that, in spite of their genuine need, shows yet again the strength of their determination to exterminate the Jews.

Still, the deportations did not always go as smoothly as the Nazis would have liked. Many Jews did not yet know or would not believe they were being taken to their deaths, but still they did not believe the lies; others knew the truth. So they hid, wherever and however they could—in chimneys, in sewers, false closets, in holes dug in the ground. The Nazi raiders searched thoroughly and carefully. Here, for instance, are some recommendations made after a roundup somewhere in Russia:

"The forces assigned to the rounding up absolutely must have axes, hatchets or similar instruments, since almost all the doors, etc., are bolted or locked and can only be forced."

If the Jews had hidden, another suggestion was made:

"A large number of people may be found in the little space between the floor and the ground. In such places it is advisable to lift the flooring from the outside and send in police dogs . . . or to throw in a grenade, which inevitably forces the Jews out of their holes."

If everything else failed, "It is recommended that adolescents be promised their lives if they help uncover the hiding places. This method is always effective." Then they were taken too.

But often enough, as in Zamosc, the Nazis did not bother to spread a fake story. They surrounded the ghetto with armed guards and appeared suddenly, with no warning. The result was, as so often with the Nazis, a bloody one. A Zamosc inhabitant recalled:

"The spectacle the ghetto presented after the attack drove the survivors mad. Bodies everywhere, in the streets, in the courtyards, inside the houses; babies thrown from third or fourth floors lay crushed on the sidewalks. The Jews themselves had to bury the dead."

THE JEWISH COUNCILS AND JEWISH POLICE

Nazi orders were passed to the ghetto through the Jewish Councils. The councils were held responsible for running the ghettos in absolute obedience to Nazi regulations and demands.

Before the deportations began, the councils made it possible for the ghettos to function in an organized way. Now, as the machinery of the Final Solution began to operate, they were told to fill the quotas of Jews demanded for each deportation. In the Warsaw ghetto the quota grew until the council was required to select six thousand Jews a day. At one point the number grew to ten thousand. The council made up a list of those to go. The Jewish police aided in the roundups, sometimes with the help of local non-Jewish police or Nazi-recruited volunteers.

The question of why the Jewish members of the councils could "serve" the Nazis in this way is a complicated one. It must be remembered that before this time, absolutely no one in the ghettos ever dreamed that the Nazis wanted to exterminate the Jews. Such a thought was almost impossible to any civilized, sane human being. As bad as life in the ghetto was, and as terrible as the Nazis' demands became, the possibility of huge masses of Jews being shipped to their deaths had never entered anyone's mind.

Assembling for deportation at the Warsaw ghetto.

Children from the Lodz ghetto orphanage board the train.

Many of these men suffered terrible agonies over the need to enforce Nazi demands. Each time some brutal order came through, doubtless some believed they were helping to save Jews from an even worse fate. Some, no doubt, simply enjoyed their power. Even when they knew the truth, many believed that by handing over the demanded quota of Jews to the Nazis, they were saving the rest.

All knew that they and their families would be killed if they did not obey, along with hundreds of other innocent Jews held hostage for their refusal. As the size of the quotas grew, and as the selection of those to be deported became more terrible—children under ten and adults over sixty-five, for example—some of these men committed suicide or voluntarily went with their families for deportation.

In the larger ghettos, such as Warsaw, orders were enforced by volunteer Nazi help and the Jewish police. It cannot be denied that some of the Jewish police were almost as cruel as the Nazis themselves, relishing a power they did not realize was temporary. They brutally assisted in the roundups for deportation.

The same questions apply to them as to the Jewish Councils. Why did they do it? How could they do it? If they did not obey Nazi orders, they would be shot—that certainly was one reason. Their wives and children

German Jews report for deportation. Unlike those to the east, Jews in Western Europe were sometimes transported in passenger cars to keep up the deception that they were being "resettled for work" and would be treated well. The cars are visible in the rear of the photograph.

were exempt from deportation, unless they failed to meet the quota assigned to them. As he wrenched a screaming child from its desperate parent, a Jewish policeman was asked how any human being could act this way. Here was his response:

"What makes you think I'm human? Maybe I'm a wild beast. I have a wife and three children. If I don't deliver my five heads by five o'clock, they'll take my own children. Don't you see? I'm fighting for my own children!"

So there are no simple answers. Deciding whether these people were good or bad is very difficult to do. Perhaps no one should make that judgment. They were forced to make decisions that few in history had to make before. They had to choose who would live and who would die from among their own people. If they chose not to obey such orders, they knew they had made another choice at the same time. They would be killed, knowing that their wives and children would also be murdered as a result of their refusal to obey.

In the end it did not matter what they did. Jews were Jews. The council members and the Jewish police met the same fate as all the others.

THE TRAINS

By order of SS Chief Heinrich Himmler, the trains carrying the deportees were considered more important than other trains. The trips from the ghettos and deportation centers involved the coordination of literally hundreds of thousands of miles of railway track, thousands of railway cars, the development of tight schedules and the use of much manpower.

This huge and complicated machinery was established and kept in motion primarily by one man: SS Lieutenant Colonel Adolf Eichmann,

The Nazis allowed no food in the ghetto for three days. Then they announced that all who reported voluntarily for "resettlement" would be given bread.

Bureau IVB-4 of the Department of Jewish Affairs. He and his representatives had been given the power to keep the trains moving under any and all circumstances. Even officials with higher rank had to give way to the demands of Eichmann's department. Himmler had given him that power, and Himmler's authority came directly from Adolf Hitler himself. Himmler had said, "The important thing to me now, as ever, is that as many Jews as humanly possible be removed to the east. I wish to be kept constantly informed . . . how many Jews have been removed each month and how many are left at that point."

And so the trains, filled with their Jewish cargo, continued their journeys to the camps.

The timetables, with their arrival and departure times, looked like any other railroad timetable. All trains were identified the same way, except that the Jewish transports were marked with a DA for those coming from out-

To Treblinka.

side Poland, and a PK or PJ for those from the General Government. The station stops were printed no differently from other stations: Chelmno, Treblinka, Auschwitz . . .

The railway companies in each country charged the SS for carrying the Jews, just as they would for any other passengers. The German railroad offered a special reduced fare for groups of four hundred or more. Children under ten went half-fare. Those under four went free. These were one-way fares. The guards on the trains were charged round-trip fares.

The fare was for passengers, but the Jews traveled in freight cars.

These cars officially could hold 8 horses or 40 soldiers. One hundred twenty to 130 men, women and children were packed into each one.

The doors were sealed shut. There was no room to sit or lie down. There was no food, no water and no heat for the journey, which could last for several days in the coldest time of the year. If there was any light at all, it came through a small opening covered with bars or barbed wire. In the winter, many froze to death before they arrived. In the summer, thirst and suffocating heat ended lives. The filth and the stench were indescribable. Some prayed, some screamed, some were silent, some went mad. A train carrying a thousand Jews would arrive—on time as scheduled—with as many as two hundred already dead.

Trains came from all over Europe, almost one right after another. Even when Germany was losing the war, trains meant for men and ammunition were used to ship Jews instead.

The Nazis congratulated one another. Here is a part of a letter from Karl Wolff, chief of Himmler's personal staff, to an official at the Transportation Ministry:

"With particular joy, I noted your assurance that for two weeks now a train has been carrying, every day, 5,000 members of the Chosen People to Treblinka, so that now we are in a position to carry through this population movement at an accelerated speed.

"I thank you again . . . and I would be grateful if you would continue to give to these things your continued personal attention."

8

THE CAMPS

I am of the opinion that bronze tablets should be laid, recording that we had the courage to carry out this great and so necessary a task.
—Odilo Globocnik, SS Chief of Lublin Police,
Director of Operation Reinhard

ARRIVAL

"THE WAGON DOORS WERE THROWN AJAR. The shouts were deafening. SS men with whips and half-wild Alsatian dogs swarmed all over the place. Uncontrolled fear brought panic as families were ruthlessly torn apart. Parents screamed for lost children and mothers shrieked their names over the voices of the bawling guards."

They were herded to the end of the train platform, where they formed two large columns, men on one side, women and children on the other. One by one they marched past two doctors. Then and there, the first selection was made. Rudolf Hoess, commander of Auschwitz, described the procedure:

"We had two SS doctors on duty at Auschwitz to examine incoming transports of prisoners. These would be marched by one of the doctors, who would make spot decisions as they walked by. Those who were fit to work were sent into the camp. Others were sent immediately to the extermination plants. Children of tender years were invariably exterminated since because of their youth they were unable to work."

Those sent to the right lived for a few more days, or weeks, or months. Those sent to the left did not. A survivor of Auschwitz described the arrival procedure this way:

"I had the opportunity to see the infamous Dr. Mengele at his macabre game of doling out life and death with his forefinger. Like a metronome this finger swayed from side to side as each victim appeared before him, with a

The stone quarry at Mauthausen, one of the earliest concentration camps. Inmates carried heavy stones on their backs up "the steps of death." Dozens died each day.

face molded in ice, without a flicker of an eyelash. Only the finger was alive, an organism itself, possessed of a strange power; it spelled out its ghastly message. . . .

"When it came [the children's] turn to stand before this automaton, they stretched out their pitiful arms and pleaded and beseeched, 'Please, Herr General. Look how strong I am. I can work. I want to live. See how strong.' But the calculating machine in human guise swung the finger to the left. They all went to the gas chambers. German economy had no use for the efforts of a twelve-year-old."

The victims selected for immediate extermination were not only the very young. Those declared unfit for life also included the old, those who looked sick, cripples and pregnant women. "Accidents" happened too; sometimes young, healthy men and women were sent to the gas chambers as well.

So, then, the ones not sent to the gas chambers immediately were the lucky ones, the ones allowed to live. But how lucky were they, what kind of life would they lead, if this was their first sight of Auschwitz:

"Corpses were strewn all over the road; bodies were hanging from the barbed-wire fence; the sound of shots rang in the air continually. Blazing flames shot into the sky; a giant smoke cloud ascended above them. Starving, emaciated human skeletons stumbled toward us, uttering incoherent sounds. They fell down right in front of our eyes. . . . "

THE IMPOSSIBLE

It may not be possible to write about the camps.

If one has never been in the camps and survived them, but has only read about them, what happens after a while is that all the words blend into one scene of Hell. The words do not, they cannot, describe what happened there.

It is possible to describe scenes of torture, to tell of cruelties meant to humiliate, cause unbearable pain or to kill. The operations of the camp can

The electrified fence at Auschwitz.

be put down in a diagram. An average day's activities can be broken down into a schedule.

But the experience of being there, of living through the life of these camps, can never be made real to those who did not experience it.

A survivor has said:

"Just as our hunger is not the feeling of missing a meal, so our way of being cold has need of a new word. We say 'hunger,' we say 'tiredness,' 'fear,' 'pain,' we say 'winter,' and they are different things . . . If the [camps] had lasted longer, a new, harsh language could express what it means to toil the whole day in the wind, with the temperature below freezing, and wearing only a shirt, underpants, cloth jacket and trousers, and in one's body nothing but weariness, hunger, and the knowledge of the end drawing near."

This was not only killing machinery. Not only planned death by gassing or gunshot, working people to death, death by torture, by starvation. The people who lived in these camps—and lived in the midst of filth, death and decay, starving, surrounded by disease and themselves sick—they lived knowing that surviving another day was absolutely a matter of chance.

Only chance prevented them from being part of the selection for that day's quota of those to be killed. Only chance kept them from being beaten to death for a reason that was no reason at all; from being shot at for target practice; from the exhausted collapse that meant automatic murder at the hands of the nearest guard; from the sickness that made them instant candidates for the gas chambers.

What happened in the camps is beyond the human imagination to describe.

But the camps were real, they existed. Millions of people died in them. Others barely survived them. For that reason the attempt to tell about them must be made. First, in memory of those who did not survive. Second, to make absolutely certain that nothing like them ever appears on the face of the earth again.

PURPOSES

The first concentration camps probably came into being because the existing jails were too small to hold the large number of people arrested by the

Separated into columns of men and women, they waited for the selection to begin. The SS men in front were doctors who decided who lived and who went to the gas chamber.

Nazis. Dachau, for instance, opened in 1933, Hitler's first year in power.

Theodor Eicke, commander of the camp and eventually of all camp guards, set the tone for Dachau and for the next twelve years when he said, "Comrades of the SS: You all know what the Führer has called upon us to do. We haven't come here to treat these swine inside like human beings. In our eyes they're not like us. . . . Any man in our ranks who can't stand the sight of blood doesn't belong here, he should get out. The more of these bastards we shoot, the fewer we'll have to feed."

The five other major camps in Germany and its neighbor Austria—Buchenwald, Sachsenhausen, Flossenburg, Mauthausen and Ravensbrück, the women's camp—all began operation in the years before the war.

The first inmates were political prisoners, opponents of the regime; Jews arrested before 1938 were among them. They were joined by the so-called asocials, which meant anyone the Nazis thought unfit for civilized society. These included habitual criminals, homeless street people, Gypsies, prostitutes and those who refused to work. After that came the nonconformists, such people as homosexuals and Jehovah's Witnesses. The latter were a danger because their religion did not allow them to join any country's armed forces.

Each inmate was given a number, which was worn on a patch sewn to his or her clothes. In some camps the number was tattooed on the prisoner's left arm. A color-coded triangle indicated the category of prisoner. Political prisoners wore red, asocials black. Pink was for homosexuals. Jehovah's Witnesses wore purple. Green was the color for habitual criminals; the most incorrigible of those were put in positions of authority over the others. In the early years Jews were placed in one of these categories; their uniforms were marked with a triangle of the appropriate color placed over a yellow triangle, to form the six-pointed Star of David.

The first mass arrest of Jews because they were Jews occurred after Kristallnacht in 1938. The 30,000 sent to the camps were released, if they survived, when their families paid the necessary amount and managed to acquire immigration papers for them. All released prisoners were sworn to secrecy, with threats to the families and themselves, about conditions in the camps and what they had suffered there.

The start of the war brought huge numbers of new prisoners to the

Families were separated.

The entrance to Birkenau, the death camp at Auschwitz.

camps. Prisoners of war, Polish professionals, anti-Nazis, members of the resistance and so on. New camps had to be built. Many of these had dozens of smaller camps attached to them, where conditions were as bad as if not worse than at the main camp. Dachau had 168, for instance, and Buchenwald 133. By the end of 1942 there were 16 main camps and thousands of smaller ones, and others continued to be built until the last year of the war. By that time in Poland alone, there were at least 6,000 camps, large and small. The map on page 55 shows only the most important camps.

SLAVE LABOR

With the war, the camps turned into a huge slave-labor enterprise. Every camp had an SS industry attached to it, some of which had begun before the war. Mauthausen had its stone quarry; Ravensbrück its textiles; Auschwitz had fish-breeding and experimental plant-growing facilities, along with an SS armaments factory.

In addition to using inmate labor in their own industries, the SS "hired out" prisoners to private German industry. Representatives on occasion came to the camps to select their laborers themselves. For working them to death on starvation rations, the industrialists paid four to six reichsmarks a day per worker—

The unfit.

approximately $2.40 to $3.60. I. G. Farben, which employed over 2,000 slave laborers, paid four reichsmarks or $2.40 for skilled labor, three reichsmarks or $1.80 for unskilled labor, and one and a half reichsmarks or $.90 for a child.

Some of the industries are still well-known names today. Besides I. G. Farben, among them are: Porsche, Krupp, Siemens, Bayer, Telefunken.

The ghettos in Eastern Europe were considered temporary holding areas for Jewish forced labor. In addition to these, all over Eastern Europe and occupied Russia hundreds of forced-labor camps were set up just for Jews. There were 125 in the General Government alone.

Strictly speaking, these were not concentration camps, although conditions were as bad and sometimes worse. A construction site would be called a labor camp even though the Jews working there had no barracks and slept on the ground; they were fed almost nothing and had only the clothes on their backs as protection against bitter cold or blasting heat. If they hesitated or fainted from exhaustion, they were beaten to death for "refusal to work." The laborers here, as well as those in the ghettos, were eventually shipped to the camps and killed—if they lived that long. The death camps themselves were built largely with Jewish forced labor.

It is true that Jews and non-Jews alike were forced to become slave laborers. But it is also true that conditions for the Jews were deliberately made worse than for any other group. In Mauthausen, which was not a death camp, during one year the death rate among non-Jews was 2 percent a month; for the Jews, it was 100 percent. Even when their work was needed, when their labor was essential to the German war effort, they were selected to die one way or another. "Extermination through work" was official policy.

The reason was a basic, simple one. What they could produce would help win the war. But one of the primary goals of the war itself was the extermination of the Jews.

THE DEATH CAMPS

It is almost false to say that the death camps were different from the concentration camps. The extermination camps had gas chambers and many of the others did not. But, asks a historian, "What, really, is the difference if [a camp] was not classified as an extermination camp and had no gas chamber, but had special rooms for mass shootings and a level of privation so severe that prisoners died in hundreds every day?" The sadism of the guards and the administration, the brutality and starvation level of daily existence, took thousands of lives daily. In Auschwitz alone, without the use of gas, there were four hundred deaths each day one December and January.

Yet the two were truly different. The death camps, perhaps more than any other single thing in the history of the regime, show the full extent of the Nazi hatred of the Jews, and their determination to destroy them.

As mentioned earlier, the basic plans for the Final Solution were drawn up at the Wannsee Conference in January 1942, but it is obvious that the idea had been brewing for a long time before that. The mobile death vans that drove along the roads of occupied Eastern Europe and Russia, the mass shootings by the Special Action Groups, the Order Police and the army—their victims were overwhelmingly Jewish. Carbon monoxide gas was used to kill Jews for the first time in Chelmno in December 1941, one month before the conference; the experiment with Zyklon B at Auschwitz had taken place even before that, in the summer. Heydrich himself had called the earlier killings and the ghettos "interim" or "temporary measures," supplying "practical experience of great importance." The final measure now became clear.

With the expert advice of the two men in charge of the euthanasia program, Christian Wirth and Victor Brack, six camps became killing centers. All used gas. Two—Auschwitz and eventually Chelmno—used Zyklon B, a poison originally used to kill insects and rats. The others used carbon monoxide gas piped into the chamber from a diesel motor kept running for the purpose. The six camps, all in Poland, went into operation in this order:

Chelmno	December 1941
Auschwitz	February 1942
Belzec	March 1942
Sobibor	April 1942
Treblinka	July 1942
Maidanek	September 1942

Three—Belzec, Sobibor and Treblinka—were built especially for Operation Reinhard, the killing of all the Jews in Poland.

The entrance to the Auschwitz main concentration camp. The sign over the gate reads WORK MEANS FREEDOM.

FROM ARRIVAL TO DISPOSAL

The arrivals platform and buildings were set up so that the victims would not know what was about to happen. From the outside they were hidden by trees. Those arriving were given the impression that they were at a temporary transit camp or labor camp until they were actually inside the gas chambers. With their dummy showerheads, these were made to resemble bathing rooms.

The entire enterprise—from arrival to disposal—happened as quickly as possible. The victims were rushed from the trains through all the steps until the end. It helped keep up an element of shock, and that prevented them from thinking about what was really happening. It disorganized them, so that they would obey all orders without resistance. The more confused and less resistant they were, the easier the job of the SS men.

The sequence of events was short and simple. The trains were emptied of their human cargo, the baggage was stacked in piles, and the selection of those to remain alive was made. Sometimes there was no selection, and all arrivals went straight to the gas chambers.

The victims then moved, often at a run, to another area. There they were told to undress. Willingly or forced, they went into the gas chambers. The heavy door was sealed shut, and in minutes all were suffocated.

Some of the Jews who had been selected to live took the bodies from the gas chambers. They were ordered to remove any remaining jewelry and gold teeth, to search and sort clothes and baggage, to cut off the women's hair. These and other Jews, with their bare hands or with wheeled carts, then moved the bodies to the pits. In the early years, the bodies were buried in mass graves; later, they were burned. In Auschwitz and some of the concentration camps like Buchenwald, large ovens designed for that use cremated the dead. The loading of the ovens and the removal of the ashes were also done by the Jews who had been allowed to live.

Eventually they too were killed, and other young, healthy Jews from other transports took their place.

TRICKS TO DECEIVE

Signs in several languages were put up in all the camps. At Chelmno they read TO THE PHYSICIAN and TO THE WASHROOM. At Belzec they said WASHING AND INHALATION EQUIPMENT. Numbered hooks were fixed to the wall at Auschwitz, with benches lined up below.

Treblinka, which was the last of the three death camps specially built for Operation Reinhard, had the most complex devices of deception. The arrival point looked like a train station—complete with clock (whose hands never moved), waiting room, ticket counter and train schedules. Those who could not move fast enough—cripples, the very old, invalids—were sent to a building where a Red Cross flag flew and a sign read INFIRMARY. They entered a waiting room with upholstered chairs, went through another door to the outside, were shot in the neck and thrown into a ditch.

A large Star of David was painted on the front wall of the building housing the gas chambers. The heavy curtain screening the door, taken from a synagogue, bore a Hebrew inscription that read, "This Is the Gateway to God. Only the Righteous Shall Enter."

As if this were not enough, sometimes the victims were given a towel and soap by white-coated guards before they entered the gas chambers.

Children might be given candy. The guards would become actors, call the victims "ladies and gentlemen," "madam" and "sir." They explained that the "showers" were a necessary health measure, told them that they would be given food afterward.

The games of deception were without limits in all the death camps. A survivor of Auschwitz recalled the speech given by an SS officer to a group of Greek Jews as they stood in the changing room at the doors of the gas chamber:

"On behalf of the camp administration I bid you welcome.

"This is not a holiday resort but a labor camp. Just as our soldiers risk their lives at the front to gain victory for the Third Reich, you will have to work here for the welfare of a new Europe. How you tackle this task is entirely up to you. The chance is there for every one of you.

"We shall look after your health, and we shall also offer you well-paid work. After the war we shall assess everyone according to his merits and treat him accordingly.

"Now, would you please all get undressed. Hang your clothes on the hook we have provided and please remember the number [of the hook]. When you've had your bath there will be a bowl of soup and coffee or tea for all."

The performance usually worked as it was supposed to. The survivor went on: "Quiet as lambs they undressed without having to be shouted at or beaten. . . . After a very short time the yard was empty except for shoes, clothing, underwear, and suitcases and boxes which were strewn all over the ground. . . . Deceived, hundreds of men, women and children had walked, innocently and without a struggle, into the large, windowless chamber."

The deception worked most effectively with victims from Western Europe. Jews there had heard nothing of the gassings; rumors had not reached them. Some had been deported to ghettos for a short stay before their final journey. But many had little direct experience with the bloody behavior of the Nazis. Attempts to trick them often began when they reported for "resettlement." Sometimes they were shipped to the death camps in passenger cars; they were even fed on the train—"from the dining car," they were told. Most believed what they had been told, that they were on their way to some area "in the East" where they would work and conditions would be much better. On the whole, they presented few problems to the smooth operation of the death camps.

But often the Jews of Poland and Eastern Europe had to be handled differently. They had lived through the ghettos and survived the terrible trip in the sealed freight cars. Many knew or suspected the truth, and the SS realized that. They were not greeted with calming speeches but by shouts and confusion. They were violently rushed out of the cars, shouted at from every side in a language they did not understand, and with whips and clubs were beaten through the steps leading to their extermination.

Whether quietly or with the help of guns and clubs, the end result was the same. "When the last one had crossed the threshold [of the gas chamber], two SS men shut the heavy iron door which was fitted with a rubber seal and locked it."

At the command of an SS officer, the crystals of Zyklon B were dropped through openings in the roof or the diesel engine brought to roaring life. It took five minutes to three-quarters of an hour for the gas to do its work.

THE NUMBERS

The exact number of victims killed at each camp will never be known, because the SS did not record the individual people who went straight from train to gas chamber. The approximate number killed at each of the six death camps is given here. The column at the right is the number of known survivors.

CAMP	VICTIMS	SURVIVORS
Chelmno	60,000	3
Belzec	600,000	2
Sobibor	250,000	64
Treblinka	900,000	Under 40
Maidanek	500,000	Under 600
Auschwitz	1,100,000	Several thousand, because it was both a concentration camp and a death camp

Nazi Economics

The intention was not only to get rid of the Jews. The Nazis also wanted to make a profit from their murder as well. Plans were carefully drawn up to make sure this would happen.

Whenever possible, the extermination machinery was made to pay for itself. So, for example, the railways billed Eichmann's department for taking Jews to the camps, and the bill was paid from the sale of stolen Jewish property. Jews helped build the camps. They worked in SS industries, and the SS was paid for their work in private industry. Jewish carpenters, electricians, plumbers and the like did most of the necessary work in the camps themselves.

Some were used as *sonderkommandos*—special commandos. They could number as many as three hundred men or more. They met the arriving transports and took the victims' baggage. They took care of the bodies from gas chamber to ashes or burial pits, and were responsible for keeping the entire killing area in tiptop running order. If they survived and did not commit suicide, then sooner or later they were shot or gassed and another group of men was chosen to carry out the same tasks.

The clothing and baggage left behind by the victims went to large sorting sheds. In Auschwitz the three enormous buildings used for this purpose were called "Canada" by inmates and SS alike. No one knows exactly why; it was located about two miles from the main camp, and perhaps it seemed as strange, far away and rich—"You could find anything there"—as that large country none of them knew.

When the killing operation was at its height, the huge warehouses would be practically filled; Auschwitz's thirty-five storage rooms were stocked to the ceilings. Two or three thousand Jews, mostly women, searched every article for hidden valuables. Even toothpaste tubes were squeezed empty in case some precious stones were hidden inside.

Everything was sorted and put in its special place. Outer clothing and underwear went here, wearable shoes there. Eyeglasses in one place, pots and pans in another. Pipes, pens, books, wallets, watches—nothing was to be wasted. Food was to be turned in immediately.

Whipping was the least punishment for taking anything out of "Canada." Yet assignment to work there was much desired. At great risk, inmates smuggled items for bribery or barter into the main camp. Food they often would eat immediately. Small objects went into their armpits or between their thighs. They wore smuggled clothing under their prison dress, carried things inside their sleeves and pants legs, hid precious stones inside their mouths. They were among the luckiest prisoners in the camp. They were better fed and looked it, and what they took from "Canada" made them rich by camp standards.

All the material taken from the Jews went for Germany's use. Money, gold and most valuables went to a special account in the main German bank. Watches, pens and wallets in good condition were sold or given as gifts to wounded soldiers. Clothes in bad condition were bundled, weighed and sold as rags. Women's hair was collected, cleaned and woven into glove and sock liners for submarine crews. Clothes in good condition were sold, "at a reasonable price," to several civilian relief organizations inside and outside Germany.

The clothes created some problems. When several thousand suits and dresses were delivered to the German Winter Aid organization, officials there complained that "most of the clothing is stained, and covered in places with filth and blood spots." In a shipment of two hundred dresses, "the Jewish Star had not been removed from 51 of them." They were given a reduced price.

Of course the Nazis stole. The temptation was too much for what Himmler called the "decent, loyal men" of the SS. They did not always have to steal. Under certain circumstances they could request an item, such as a gold pen or leather boots of a certain size. This was permitted for the sake of their morale, as extra payment for the "hazardous and difficult duty" of working in the camps.

No one will ever know how much they stole. Nor will anyone ever know the full value of this pillage of the dead. The material taken from Operation Reinhard alone was estimated at 180 million reichsmarks—approximately $128 million. Its true value was probably several times greater than that.

The Nazis were officially instructed to call Jewish property "goods stolen, concealed, and hoarded by the Jews." Himmler said, "The riches they had we have taken from them." Whatever they called it, however they described it, Himmler would have spoken the honest truth if he had said, "We have taken everything they owned."

9

LIFE IN THE CAMPS

We were forced to come to the grim decision that this
people must be made to disappear from the face of
the earth . . . . We have tackled [the assignment] and
carried it through without our men and our leaders
suffering any damage in their minds and souls.
—Heinrich Himmler, Supreme Leader of the SS

JEWS WHOSE LIVES WERE SPARED AT THE DEATH CAMPS worked at the killing
machinery until they too were killed. Jews sent to the concentration camps,
which included the main camp at Auschwitz, were also spared to work for
as long as they could survive. Their introduction to camp life was a carefully
worked out, step-by-step procedure.

THE INTRODUCTION

The chaos of the arrival and the first selection on the platform had a purpose;
it was planned. The SS men "had to set out to break our morale, to wipe out
every trace of human feeling, to drive fear, dread and panic into us. The spine-
chilling terror infused in us at the very moment of our arrival never left us."

The moving finger had pointed some toward life, at least for a while,
even if they did not know it then. Shouting guards with rifle butts and clubs
marched the separate groups of men and women into the camp. At the
entrance to Auschwitz, they passed under the huge gate with its inscription,
ARBEIT MACHT FREI—Work Means Freedom. At Buchenwald, the inscription
read, *JEDEM DAS SEIN*—Each Gets What He Deserves.

Bullied, some bleeding, constantly yelled at, they were put into an
unheated room and told to undress. Their bags and bundles had been taken
from them on the arrival platform. Now their clothes would be taken from
them as well. Dresses, suits, jackets, went into one place, shoes in another.
Rings, watches, jewelry and money were put in piles of their own.

Women selected for work. They have gone through the first steps of life in the camp and soon will be sent to their block.

SS men came and went, shouting orders. Other prisoners, wearing arm-bands, carried sticks and hit out mercilessly if anyone hesitated or asked a question. The women suffered the double humiliation of being naked in front of the men's eyes.

Soon prisoner barbers appeared—many had been barbers or hairdressers in their earlier lives. Men's heads and beards were shaved with dull razors. Women's hair was clipped close to the skull, dropping in heaps to the floor. Their armpits and other body hair were shaved.

"We really had nothing now except our bare bodies—even minus hair. All we possessed, literally, was our naked existence."

With shouts and blows they moved on to the showers—real showers, if the trickle of ice-cold water could be called that. There was no soap, no towel, and the water stopped after a few moments.

Still naked and shivering, they were then "disinfected," deloused with a sticky, foul-smelling blue liquid.

Accompanied by more blows, more shouts, they were driven into another room and given clothes at last. They did not know then that these were the clothes of others who had been killed only shortly before. One would get pants so large they had to be held up, a shirt so small it would not button. A woman might get a long silk dress or a pair of riding jodhpurs. For their feet they received wooden clogs; too small or too large made no difference. Eventually in most of the camps they were given uniforms of rough cloth; in many the uniforms were striped.

Immediately after this, they were given their numbers. In Auschwitz, the number was tattooed in blue on the left forearm. That was all they would be from now on—their number. If they were to eat and drink, have a place to sleep, if they were not to be beaten or shot for not knowing it, this number was all that they were here.

A survivor, age seventeen at the time, remembered that the camp leader came to them and said just that: "From now on you have no identity. You have no place of origin. All you have is a number. Except for the number you have nothing."

"In a moment," another survivor wrote, "the reality was revealed to us: we had reached bottom. It is not possible to sink lower than this, nor could it conceivably be so. Nothing belongs to us anymore; they have taken away our clothes, our shoes, even our hair; if we speak, they will not listen to us, and if they listen, they will not understand. They will even take away our name. . . . "

DAILY LIFE

An SS commander named Krause on a visit to Auschwitz noticed a low number on an inmate's arm, which meant he had been there for a long while. Krause said, "A prisoner should not survive more than six weeks in a concentration camp. If he lives beyond that time, it simply means he has adapted and must be liquidated immediately."

His comment, along with the events of arrival and introduction to the camp, reveal clearly that almost everything that happened was planned.

Almost every element of camp life had been designed beforehand to break down each inmate in body and in mind.

If the prisoner did not starve, then he would die of disease. If he did not die of disease, then he would be murdered by some action of camp personnel—a beating, a "game" or deliberate murder. If that did not finish him, then work beyond all strength would take him. Last, if none of these destroyed him, then the regular selection for the gas chambers would be the end of him.

The camps were not places to live. They were deliberately established to be places to die.

The barracks were called blocks. Meant for five hundred, they held two thousand. Four or five people slept on each bunk, head to foot. The "mattress" was filthy straw on bare wooden planks. One or two buckets served as toilets.

Prisoners were awakened at four o'clock in the morning or earlier. Rushed out into the field, they lined up in rows of five and roll call began. Numbers had to match the record. If so much as one person was missing, roll call could last three, ten, even twenty-four hours. Those who had died during the night had to make their appearance too, and their bodies were dragged onto the field for the count.

Standing in their ragged clothes, many of the starved, sick, weak inmates dropped where they stood. In this way roll call was a selection as well. If a guard or supervisor thought the line was not straight enough, or did not like the way a man's hat fit on his head or that a woman was wearing a kerchief that day—in other words, for reasons that were no reasons—those prisoners would be punished, beaten or possibly shot.

Most labor was outside the camp area. At Auschwitz and other camps, the inmates marched to work to the sounds of an orchestra. Some of Europe's best musicians were there as inmates. Each morning and evening, they were forced to play marches, and the prisoners were ordered to step out to work and back to camp in precise military rhythm.

The work was supervised by *kapos*—leaders—picked from among the prisoners. Kapos were usually Jews who sought favor from the SS by brutal enforcement of all work orders. They might also be non-Jews, habitual criminals or murderers. They were rewarded with better food and living quarters. But if a kapo was thought to be "soft" or if the work group did not meet expectations, he or she could expect to meet the same fate as the other prisoners.

Bunks in Auschwitz. Three to five slept on each. The "mattress" was filthy straw.

The work was backbreaking and physically destructive. If that were not enough, some kapos forced the inmates to work at a run or beat them mercilessly. As many as half a work group would die on any given day. Others, near collapse, would be helped to the entrance of the camp by their fellow inmates. But once at the gates, they would snap upright and march in rhythm into the camp to the strains of the music, in time for another roll call.

Disease ran rampant. They were given no change of clothes and were rarely if ever permitted to wash. The lice and fleas caused by the inescapable filth brought the typhus and dysentery that took the lives of thousands. All camps had hospitals, often staffed by prisoners who had been doctors and nurses. But these were not white-coated dispensers of medicine and health. With thousands of patients in the hospital block, they might be given two or three hundred aspirin. In many camps the hospitals were places to be dreaded; selection for the gas chambers were made there more often than elsewhere, because the time it took to get well was time spent not working.

Not only conditions and disease took their toll. So also did what the prisoners and guards called "sport." Inmates, usually the most feeble, would be made to do knee bends and push-ups in the filthy mud and were flogged or shot when they dropped. They would have to hold heavy stones over their heads until permitted to put them down, and be beaten if their arms sagged or the stones fell. Two or three Jews would be ordered to play "tag"; the ones tagged would be killed for losing the game. SS guards would use Jews for target practice, aiming at the fingers or the nose, and then kill them because they were no longer fit for work.

Their food—watery saltless soup made with rotten vegetables and tainted meat, a few ounces of bread and "tea"—was not fit to eat, except by the already starving. And so hunger, hunger above all, was the greatest torment. It was constant, as much a part of their bodies as their bones. They would eat grass—and be beaten if they were caught—steal crusts of bread from the bodies of dead inmates. Hunger formed the foundation of each moment of their lives in the camps. It did not take long for that to happen.

"A fortnight after my arrival," a survivor wrote, "I already had the prescribed hunger, that chronic hunger unknown to free men, which makes one

One of the gas chambers.

dream at night, and settles in all the limbs of one's body. . . . On the back of my feet I already had those numb sores that will not heal. I push wagons, I work with a shovel, I turn rotten in the rain, I shiver in the wind; already my body is no longer mine: my belly is swollen, my limbs emaciated, my face is thick in the morning, hollow in the evening; some of us have yellow skin, others gray. When we do not meet each other for a few days, we hardly recognize each other."

Many died in the camps not because they were selected for the gas or for any other usual camp reason. Some, unable to bear such a life, "went to the wire"; they killed themselves by flinging their bodies against the electrified fence. Others were the living dead. For reasons no one knows, the inmates called them *Muselmänner*—German for Muslims. They had reached such a point of starved wretchedness that the light had vanished from their eyes. They did not walk, they shuffled from place to place; they did not speak. They had died inside while waiting for death, and death always came soon after that.

SELECTIONS

Selections for the gas chambers took place at more or less regular intervals. Some involved the whole camp, others just one block. Hospital selections could happen at any time.

Inmates were ordered to their blocks. One or more SS doctors, accompanied by one or two of their most favored inmates and occasionally by a few guards, appeared in the yard and went to the block chosen for that day.

Selections took place inside the block or outside in the field. Sometimes the inmates were made to run past the doctor, who pointed to the right or to the left as they passed in front of him. More often, at a shouted command from the block leader, all inmates stood sharply at attention. Frequently they were made to strip, especially the women. The doctor's inmate assistant or the block leader called out each prisoner's number from a list as he or she walked along the rows. At Auschwitz, each prisoner extended his left arm. As the doctor made his selection, that inmate's number was checked off the list.

Anyone too sick to leave his or her bunk was an automatic choice, as was anyone who collapsed or could not stand straight enough. An unhealed wound, a simple rash, illness or weakness that could not be hidden—all these were automatic sentences to selection. Here, too, as on the arrivals ramp, "mistakes" were made, and someone no less healthy than the other living skeletons in the block was pointed to the left.

Those selected were not taken then. They waited hours, sometimes days, knowing they were marked for death. Eventually they were removed to a barracks—at Auschwitz it was Block 25—where they waited again, without food or water, until a large enough number had been collected to make running the gas "economical." Sooner or later, that moment always came.

JOSEF MENGELE AND SS MEDICINE

Josef Mengele was chief medical officer in Birkenau, the Auschwitz killing center. In charge of all the camp selections, he was the most feared of all camp doctors. Handsome, always elegantly dressed in custom-tailored uniforms and wearing white gloves, he earned his nicknames of "Beautiful Devil" and "Angel of Death." He made sure to arrange a selection on every Jewish holiday. Inmates might forget a date, but he did not; they called him their "Jewish calendar."

Mengele aroused particular dread among the women. He made a habit of appearing unexpectedly in their section of the camp and always required them to strip. The sick and starving women paraded before him in the yard, arms held over their heads, while he whistled some operatic aria as he pointed to the right or to the left with his riding crop.

He paid frequent visits to the infirmary. Newcomers, mostly women, could not yet understand the truth of this place. So they were expecting medical help. Mengele sat down in a chair and charmingly coaxed each one to talk to him. Inspired to confidence by his handsomeness, they spoke freely to him about their illnesses. Smiling often, seeming to listen carefully, in easy comfort he made his selections of those unfit to work.

Before the war, Mengele had been on the staff of the Nazi-founded Institute of Hereditary Biology and Race Research. In Auschwitz he continued his "research," using inmates for his studies. He found twins particularly fascinating, so they went directly to him instead of to the gas. He wanted to learn the secret of their birth for the sake of the Third Reich, which could then use it to increase the Nazi birthrate. "He believed," said a survivor, "that you could create a new super-race as though you were breeding horses."

Mengele is remembered with exceptional hatred by survivors. But many SS doctors in the camps used inmates—"cheaper than rats"—as laboratory animals. They did so with the full approval of Berlin's Institute of Hygiene. They all did more or less the same things. They did not heal. Instead, Nazi doctors in the camps made medicine into partners with murder.

SURVIVAL

It is almost unbelievable that any Jews lived through the camps. Yet some did survive. Maybe they escaped selection or a killing beating or disease by luck or by accident. But it was neither luck nor accident that helped them get through.

Camp regulations were designed to make life impossible. If an inmate was to live, some way had to be found to get around them. And ways were found. The same word was used in all the camps to describe what was done: "organize." A survivor defined it best:

"The most important word in the Auschwitz language: 'organization' was the key to survival. It meant to steal, buy, exchange, get hold of. Whatever you wanted, you had to have something to barter for it. Some people spent every waking moment 'organizing': stealing from their fellow prisoners, bribing others, swapping a crust of bread for a can of water, a crumpled sheet of note paper for a more comfortable corner of a bunk."

If they were caught with anything they were not supposed to have, it meant at least a beating. In spite of this they bartered, bribed, bought, stole, exchanged such things as a piece of warm clothing, a pair of shoes, a blanket, a needle and thread, even bowls and spoons without which they could not eat.

At Auschwitz, prisoners assigned to work in "Canada" sneaked in small items of food or pieces of clothing. Jewelry and gold found its way into the main camp (paper money was used as toilet paper). Prisoners who worked in potato fields would smuggle one, two, whatever they could hide. Inmates who labored outside the camp might have contact with some civilian they could bribe. Even some SS guards could be "bought."

But mostly it was the small things, items that in the normal world might well be thrown into the garbage without a thought. Things like these could make the difference between life and death, even if for only just that one day.

All the survivors talk about the close attachments they formed. "Loners" did not last very long. "Help one another," an Auschwitz inmate said to a newcomer. "It is the only way to survive." Risking his or her own life, a prisoner would help hide a sick fellow inmate during a selection. The meager food ration would be shared with a particularly weak prisoner. A flower found outside the camp would be smuggled inside and given as a gift. A prisoner about to drop during a long roll call would be held upright by the tightly squeezed bodies of inmates in front and back of him.

This does not mean the camps were places of noble and unselfish behavior. They were not. Perhaps most inmates did not try to live by seeking favor from those higher up in the camp, but there were many who did. Some kapos and block leaders behaved almost as cruelly as the SS themselves. Others lied, cheated, stole whenever and however they could, from sick or sleeping fellow prisoners.

All prisoners had to think of themselves first. To survive meant to be completely selfish. "Here," an inmate explained, "there are no fathers, no brothers, no friends. Everyone lives and dies for himself alone." They "organized" and fought for the sake of their own lives above all else. If they managed to do that successfully, then—and only then—would they have the thought and the strength to help someone else. And if one prisoner did help another, he or she would usually be paid back in some other way—perhaps by nothing more than an extra crust of bread when weakness drained the strength needed to "organize."

Many survivors talk of the determination to live in order to be a witness. Despite what surrounded them, they believed Germany would lose the war. Therefore they had to remain alive to tell what had happened here. They knew that the planned destruction of human life in the camps could not be imagined by normal people in a normal world. If humanity was to know of this horror, then living witnesses had to tell the tale. Only then would justice become possible. If they told the story of that nightmare world of the camps, they would help make sure that such evil would never again take root and flourish.

"It seems odd," wrote a woman of Auschwitz, "but everyone wanted to live. In this terrible world there was room for hopes and dreams. The most beautiful images of life after the war shimmered in the mind's eye. We imagined that after the war people would be richer for the experience and would create a paradise on earth, without wars and without persecution. Is it any wonder that everyone wanted to see the defeat of Germany and the world that would come into being after that took place?"

"There were things I had to do," said another survivor, "words I had to speak . . . in order to show the world what I had seen and lived through, on behalf of the millions who had seen it also—but could no longer speak. Of their dead, burned bodies, I would be the voice."

"Some of us had to live," wrote a fifteen-year-old, "to defy them all, and one day to tell the truth."

10

FIGHTING BACK

Listen you murderers, you scum! If you should now
offer me life and happiness on condition that I give up
my faith and "become an Aryan," I would spit in your
face. Because you are murderers, the meanest animals
on earth, and we are Jews.
                                        —Ukrainian Jew to German guards,
                                                        moments before his death

I don't know who will win this war, but one thing I am
sure of—people like you, a nation like yours, will
never be defeated, never!
                                        —German soldier to Czech Jew

W HY DIDN'T THE JEWS FIGHT BACK? Did they go to their deaths "like sheep
to the slaughter," as some writers claim?

It can certainly seem as though they did. In almost every instance, Jews
being rounded up or readied for slaughter outnumbered the Nazis there to
do the job. Yet the Nazis succeeded in killing close to six million. Why was
there no resistance?

The word *resistance* used in a wartime situation usually means to oppose
actively, to fight back openly with arms and ammunition. That definition is
correct as far as it goes. But there are other ways of resisting and fighting
back. The Jews took advantage of all of them, eventually assaulting their
enemy with weapons and explosives as well.

So little is known about what they did because so few survived the attempts.
Written records are rare; some of those were found hidden under floorboards or
buried in the ground several years after the war. With only a handful of survivors
and almost no record of the time, primarily Nazi accounts have to be depended
on to tell the story. And why would they tell the truth about that?

The fact of the matter is this: the Jews fought the Nazis in all the ways
that were possible for them.

Crematorium 2 in Birkenau.

How they fought was determined by several things. First, by their history, traditions and religion, all of which spoke against open resistance. Second, by events as they happened and the circumstances surrounding them. Third, when armed resistance did occur, by the amount of assistance and ammunition they could acquire for themselves. The story of that fight appears in the next chapter.

HISTORY, TRADITIONS AND RELIGION

The Jews have a long history of persecution. Suffering of one kind or another has been their lot for almost as long as they have existed. They had learned from that, and tried to apply those lessons to their present situation.

They had been expelled from their homes and countries in the past, but they always managed to start over again and build thriving communities

The ovens in a crematorium.

elsewhere. Allowed residence only in certain areas before, they established separate and largely self-sufficient ghettos. Forbidden certain vocations, they trained in other kinds of work. Unexpected and bloody pogroms had been visited on them many times, but enough survived to restore their communities and go on living.

Governments had passed anti-Semitic laws, and Jews learned how to obey or work around them. Such governments had come—and then they had gone, and the government that eventually followed was often not so oppressive as the one before. Jews believed the Nazi regime to be a government like any other. More murderous perhaps, and crazed on the subject of Jews, but like any government its time would pass and changes for the better would come about.

So when they had their rights taken away from them and had to live as less than second-class citizens in their home country, it was a familiar experience from their own past. Prohibited from working in various professions in Germany and Nazi-controlled areas, they found other work and set up their own self-help organizations. Torn from their homes and locked into ghettos, they could remember others in their history. These new ghettos were perhaps more cruel and deadly, but those who survived—there had always been survivors—would find ways to live on.

They were accused of starting the war, of murdering little children to use their blood in Passover matzoh, of controlling the world's money. But lies had always been spread about them; they were used to that. When they were beaten or killed just because they were Jews, they had the memory of earlier pogroms to fall back on. This was more terrible than before, but those who remained would carry on, just as earlier Jews had done before them.

The Jews had not been a nation in almost two thousand years of their history; there was no such thing as a Jewish country. Because of that, they had never had their own armies. They had fought in the armies of the countries they lived in, often with great patriotism and bravery. But they had never fought as Jews in a Jewish army. Very few had any experience of armed battle. They lacked the knowledge of the techniques and had no way of acquiring the necessary supplies. They simply did not think in terms of fighting back openly.

The Jewish religion reinforced that attitude. These were a very religious people. The Eastern European Jews were especially so, but the less orthodox and those who practiced no religion at all came from the same tradition and were influenced by it.

The most devout among them did not believe that physical force could win against worldly evil. God alone could triumph, and their prayers had more power than the strongest army on earth. He alone understood why this was happening, and it was blasphemous to question Him. Many went to their deaths in joyous prayer, believing that they died a martyr's death, *Kiddush ha-Shem*—for the sake of God.

They knew death was the consequence of any act of defiance. That made such acts equivalent to suicide, and suicide was forbidden by Jewish law. Human life was the highest, holiest value. To take a life was thus among the worst possible sins. Since fighting meant to kill and even a Nazi was a human being, the Jews would not fight.

Nothing in their history—in the world's history—prepared them for the Nazi plan to exterminate all Jews wherever they were found. Equally important, they did not know of this plan until it had already begun.

EVENTS AND CIRCUMSTANCES

"Why talk about a civilian population," a survivor asks, "which had an actually large proportion of elderly persons and children, when at the same time armies of well-trained soldiers were also annihilated? The fact is, the Nazi forces smashed one army after another and succeeded in occupying almost all of Europe and parts of Africa."

Unarmed, bewildered men, women and children were faced by well-organized, heavily armed men who knew exactly what they were doing, and furthermore had been given complete freedom to commit any act of cruelty and persecution to carry it out. How much fighting back was possible under such circumstances?

In addition to men and arms, the Germans used another powerful weapon against resistance. They held each individual responsible for the behavior of the group, and the group responsible for each individual. In practice, this collective responsibility meant that many, even hundreds, would die if so much as one person tried to fight back. Countless stories show the Nazi thoroughness in carrying this out. Let two quotes from a report by a Special Action Group in Lithuania tell the story for all:

From Kovno, October 4, 1941: "315 Jewish men, 721 Jewish women, 818 Jewish children (punitive action because a German policeman was shot at in the ghetto)."

From Vilna, September 2, 1941: "864 Jewish men, 2,109 Jewish women, 817 Jewish children (special action because German soldiers were shot at by Jews)."

How could they fight, when the punishment meant the deaths of their families and friends—of hundreds of innocent people?

The Jews left in Germany hoped against hope that eventually their persecution would end. Little news of their plight had reached Eastern Europe. When the Special Action Groups followed almost at the heels of the triumphant German armies, they found a general populace still in shock at the speed of Nazi success, and Jews in particular mostly in ignorance of what to expect.

Not only surprise and lack of knowledge worked against resistance. So also did the games of deception the Nazis played. Details of these appear in an earlier chapter, but it is important to remember that the Nazis tried to deceive the Jews about their true purposes every step of the way—from calling the deportations "resettlements in the East" to the signs that read TO THE SHOWERS at the camps themselves. They went so far as to make their victims send back postcards that said they were well and working—this from the fake train station at Treblinka.

Those in the ghettos were sealed off from communication with the outside world. When news of the mass murders and death camps reached them, in general they refused to believe it. The monstrous act of extermination was beyond their imagination to comprehend. By the time they began to understand, the prisoners of camp and ghetto were weakened in body and spirit by the Nazi terror and cut off from any outside help.

And if they escaped, where would they find safety? The non-Jewish populations living near the camps and ghettos were also under the Nazi yoke. In Eastern Europe helping Jews was punishable by death. Collective responsibility held here too; whole families, even entire communities, were executed because they had hidden one Jew. In Western Europe, including Germany, the penalty was also severe: a sentence to a concentration camp.

And, sadly, much of the population had no sympathy for the Jews. That held true in almost all the affected countries; the few exceptions will be described in a later chapter. It was most obvious in parts of Eastern Europe, especially in Poland and Ukraine, whose anti-Semitic histories worked to the Nazis' benefit. Some towns and villages actually welcomed the Germans. Informers, paid for finding Jews, betrayed them everywhere. Each country supplied the SS with volunteers, including guards for the death camps. Many people sympathized with Nazi aims and would offer no assistance of any kind. Jews who managed to escape could expect little help anywhere, even from among their own countrymen.

At the first events of the early years of Nazi power, thousands left their homes and sought safety elsewhere. A large number succeeded, but many more did not go far enough and were trapped in another country by the speed of the Nazi advance through Europe. Thousands more tried to leave but could not, because no other nation would have them; they too were trapped.

So far these are all reasons for not acting, for submitting and dying without so much as a clenched fist. They weigh heavily; they help explain why resistance was not more common.

Because there certainly was resistance. Against the largest machinery of death the world had ever known, the Jews fought back in every way within their power.

SABOTAGE

Any deliberate slowdown or act of sabotage among the slave laborers in SS and German industries was punished in the usual Nazi manner. Yet they occurred numberless times in endless variations.

Slowdowns were everywhere and frequent. If the kapo or German foreman was stupid, drunk or a little less brutal than others, output would drop until it began to be noticed and then would swing back to normal again. Key people would be "too sick" to work for several days. An important piece of machinery would "break down." Coal trucks were allowed to run off the rails. Conveyor belts mysteriously caught on fire.

In sewing-repair shops, uniform sleeves were closed, buttonholes left uncut, zippers not lined up straight. Shoes were repaired with glue that dissolved in water. Sand and alcohol went into gas tanks.

French Jewish women at Auschwitz sabotaged an experiment in growing rubber-producing plants. Three-quarters of the guns made at Buchenwald were returned as defective. Of the ten thousand V-1 and V-2 rockets manufactured at Dora-Mittelbau, fewer than half reached their targets.

At Dachau, tank engines were sabotaged. At Ravensbrück, munitions and spare parts. Planes with fatal flaws came from Sachsenhausen, damaged U-boat parts from Neuengamme.

As smart as they were, the Germans never seemed to realize that slaves do not always do good work for cruel masters. They overestimated the effect of their terror, and underestimated human courage.

RESISTANCE IN DAILY LIFE

It is worth repeating: Nazi regulations were designed to make life impossible, both in the camps and in the ghettos.

To obey them meant to die sooner or later. To disobey them meant to die immediately. So they were obeyed as much as necessary. And they were disobeyed as much as possible.

The constant demands were resisted at every level. In the ghettos, those cities of the dying, a secret vibrant life went on in direct defiance of the Nazis. Despite the penalty, war was waged against starvation by smuggling food. Self-help groups were organized to aid the homeless and nurse the sick with whatever small means could be found. Here is how one survivor of the Warsaw ghetto put it:

"The Nazis demanded that the Jews hand over their money and movable possessions, but the Jews did not comply with this order. The Nazis forbade the Jews to engage in trade or work as artisans, but the Jews labored in secret and manufactured goods clandestinely. The Nazis prohibited communal prayer but the Jews gathered despite the prohibition and held services on weekdays and festivals. The Nazis forbade the Jews to open schools, but the Jews organized [secret] kindergartens and schools for all age groups. . . ."

In the camps even more than in the ghettos, all elements of daily life were meant to kill. Since that is true, it is not nonsense to say that the simple act of staying alive was a form of resistance. Survivors often mention that it took great effort not to choose "the easy way out"—death. For a Jew to live was a defiance of Nazi wishes.

But resistance went further than that. From Auschwitz:

"Our entire existence was marked by [resistance]. When the employees of 'Canada' detoured items destined for Germany to the benefit of their fellow internees, it was resistance. When laborers at the spinning mills dared to slacken their working pace, it was resistance. When . . . we organized a little 'festival' under the noses of our masters, it was resistance. When, clandestinely, we passed letters from one camp to another, it was resistance. When we endeavored, and sometimes with success, to reunite two members of the same family—for example, by substituting one internee for another in a gang of stretcher bearers—it was resistance. . . . We resisted to live, and lived to resist."

They hid women about to give birth so both mother and newborn infant would not face the automatic death sentence. They substituted a dead prisoner's number to save another selected for the gas. The religious among them rose earlier than the rest to say morning prayers and recited the prayer for the dead—the *Kaddish*—every night.

Each of these was equally an act of resistance, since all were equally forbidden. In those kingdoms of death, they took enormous courage.

REBELLION

Stories of rebellion form a part of every survivor's memory of events. Nazi records tell of others. Almost none of those involved remained alive to tell the story themselves.

In Amsterdam, Gestapo officials came across a secret meeting and were met by acid and bullets.

Shot but not dead, a Polish butcher leaped from a body-filled pit and tore out the throat of the SS commander with his teeth.

Survivors of the ghetto in a Cracow prison attacked the guards with their bare hands and seriously wounded several.

A teenager in a transport from Grodno threw a hand grenade at Treblinka guards.

A Frenchwoman grabbed an SS man's dagger and stabbed him.

Two thousand new arrivals at Sobibor tore wood from the freight cars and assaulted their captors.

Stopped by a guard from saying good-bye to his mother, the son stabbed him with his pocketknife.

Five thousand deported from Vilna found weapons and fought. Nazi records admit two guards seriously wounded, fifty Jews escaped.

A fourteen-year-old Czech leaped on the back of a guard, knocked him to the ground and beat his face bloody with his bare fists.

An old man on the way to the Sobibor gas chamber recited a prayer out loud and, when he finished, slapped the SS man's face.

Twenty-five hundred Jews from the town of Brody rebelled, broke up their deportation train and killed several guards; hundreds escaped.

One event appears in nearly all survivors' histories from Auschwitz, particularly the women's. In some she is a French dancer, in others from somewhere in Eastern Europe. The details are often different from one version to the next, but the basic meaning of the story is the same. In all she is described as very beautiful, with long black hair. Her name is not known.

A transport of prisoners pulled up at the arrivals ramp. "All of a sudden the door of our compartment opened with a loud noise and an SS man told us to strip naked and to come out to the station. . . . He started to hit us with his rifle butt.

"We had to go forward completely naked; men, women and children. The dancer . . . was the only one who did not get undressed."

She was forced to start taking off her clothes. Another witness goes on:

"The SS men were fascinated. . . . She steadied herself against a concrete pillar and bent down, slightly lifting her foot in order to take off her shoe. What happened next took place with lightning speed: quick as a flash she grabbed her shoe and slammed its high heel into [an SS man's] forehead. He winced with pain and covered his face with both hands. At this moment the young woman flung herself at him and made a quick grab for his pistol. There was a shot. [Another guard] cried out and fell to the ground. Seconds later there was a second shot . . . which missed. The third shot was fired; one of the SS men . . . started to limp to the door as fast as he could."

And finally, "She saved the last shot for herself."
But she had fought back.

ESCAPE

The deportation trains traveled at high speed. Doors were locked from the outside and often nailed shut. Alert armed guards were posted everywhere. To escape from these moving pestholes meant ripping up the floorboards and dropping to the tracks under the moving train, or squeezing through the small barbed-wire opening and stumbling hard onto the ground. If the fall did not break bones and the shooting guards missed, escape into the forest was the next step.

Many tried and died beside the tracks. Jews unused to living in the woods died there. Or they were caught, turned in and deported again. The story that follows is a typical one. He was a young boy barely in his teens, on his way to Belzec.

"I decided to escape. We were a few youngsters, and we tore down the barbed wire from the small window. I climbed to the window, squeezed myself through and jumped. It was dark, the SS guards were shooting all the time, even without seeing any escapee, just to frighten. I fell on the earth, the train passed by. . . .

"I was marching on a path, suddenly in front of me appeared a Ukrainian who shouted at me: 'Where are you going?' I answered that I was on my way to [the town of] Kolomyya. 'So you escaped from the train. Let's go to the police,' he said, and caught my hand. . . .

"I started to run. I ran as if Death were behind me, and succeeded in escaping. . . .

"I continued on my way when I found myself surrounded by three Ukrainians. They led me to a small barrack . . . where I met some other Jews who had escaped the transport and had been caught. We were beaten up. . . .

"Along the railway, many victims were lying who, like myself, had jumped from the train. Some were dead; others were still alive, but with broken hands and legs.

"In Kolomyya . . . we were again beaten up and then taken to the Gestapo and to prison."

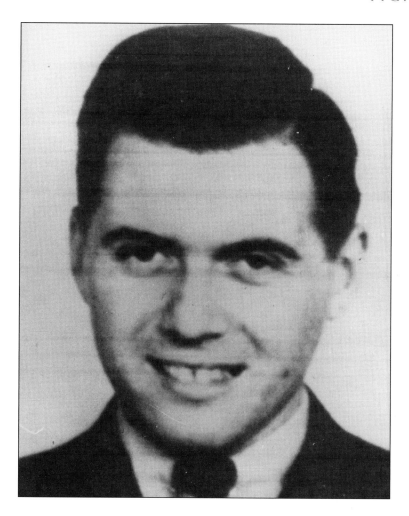

Josef Mengele, chief medical officer in Birkenau. Handsomeness combined with his enjoyment of selections and medical experiments earned him the nickname "Beautiful Devil." This photo is from his SS file.

The kinds of things that happened to that boy worked against anyone's successful escape from the trains. Some did make it, but not many. They lived out the war in hiding, eating whatever they could find in the woods, or discovered local people willing to take them in. Some found resistance groups—the partisans—in the forest and joined them to fight the Germans for as long as they could.

Escapees from the camps found similar problems if they got as far as the woods. In addition, SS men with dogs searched widely and thoroughly. Escape attempts were many—667 from Auschwitz alone during its five-year existence. Successes were few—of those 667, only 76 were known to have broken free.

*The victims' wedding rings and
shoes, all to be used for the profit
of the Third Reich.*

Not every kind of prisoner could try to break out. Most were extremely limited in their movements within the camp. They were permitted to go only from block to work to roll call and back to block; their absence would be noticed immediately. Some in higher positions, however, could move about more freely—doctors and nurses, plumbers and electricians, burial squads, messengers and the like. Most escape attempts came from among their ranks.

Breakouts occurred at each of the camps, including Belzec, Treblinka and Sobibor. The problems faced at Auschwitz were similar to all.

Escape required precise step-by-step planning. Secrecy was essential; only the absolutely trusted few were told. Supplies had to be "organized." Clothes, money and food were smuggled in, usually from "Canada," and hidden. Contact with the outside world was crucial. The occasional workers from outside who worked inside the camp, though forbidden to talk to prisoners, were the usual source of maps and information about safe routes and reliable people (they were paid well for this information).

A double row of electrified fence surrounded the camp. Armed sentries ringed the perimeter, while others watched from observation towers. The moment a prisoner was missing from roll call, the search began. If he was not found in the camp, sirens went off and dozens of SS men with their dogs, aided by local police, looked for him outside the camp, searching the ground inch by inch.

If the escapee managed to get through all this, he found himself in an area inhabited by Germans. As a safety feature, native Poles had been moved out of a thirty-square-mile area around the camp, and ethnic Germans— those of German background raised in Poland—were moved in.

Having survived this, he faced a dangerous, difficult journey on foot to where he believed he might be safe. If he was not caught by Nazi sympathizers or betrayed by those supposed to help him, he might then remain alive until some safer time.

It is amazing that anyone made it from any of the camps. Yet there were successes. Four who escaped from Auschwitz were responsible for bringing the first news of gas chambers and the Nazi extermination plan to the West. Those who joined partisan groups in the forest did more damage to the Nazis than any records will ever show. Many died in those battles and will remain unknown forever.

ALL POSSIBLE WAYS

The power brought against the Jews of Europe seemed invincible. Their friends were few, the terror endless. Nothing in their lives prepared them for this, nor could it have. Fighting actively was not natural to them. Yet they resisted in all the ways the horror of their circumstances would allow.

They were not finished yet. When they knew that extermination was to be their end, they fought as tirelessly as the bravest soldier in the most modern army. With weapons in their hands, they fought back in ways the Nazi understood.

11

ARMED RESISTANCE

The last wish of my life has been fulfilled. Jewish self-defense has become a fact. Jewish armed resistance and revenge have become realities.
—Mordechai Anielwicz, leader of the Warsaw Ghetto Jewish Combat Organization

THE FACTS

THE FACTS ARE THESE: IN EVERY ONE OF THE NAZI-CONTROLLED countries, where there were Jews there was a Jewish underground and Jewish resistance. In the ghettos, concentration camps, even in the death camps, there were armed revolts against the Nazis.

The exact number will never be known. The secrecy required at the time and the constant danger of capture meant that written records were rarely kept, or else were hidden and have not yet been found. The few survivors grow fewer with the years, and their memories die with them.

Still, it is known that the twenty-five episodes shown on the map on page 124 reflect only part of the story. Today, interviews with survivors and research continue tirelessly, to learn as much of the whole story as possible before all traces vanish with time.

So far it is known that in central Poland there were three armed rebellions and four attempted rebellions. Armed resistance groups existed in seventeen different places. Evidence has been found in western Belorussia of ninety-one armed underground groups.

But what of it? Why does Jewish resistance matter? After all, the Nazis almost succeeded in doing what they had set out to do. They lost the war in the end, but not before they had killed most of Europe's Jews. So if success is measured only by the defeat of an enemy, then Jewish resistance was a failure.

121

Mordechai Anielwicz, the leader of the Warsaw
ghetto uprising.

But the episodes are successes in another way. The Jews fought realisti-
cally, without hope of winning. A leader of the Bialystok ghetto resistance
put it this way: "If we are too weak to safeguard our lives, we are still strong
enough to defend the honor of the Jew and of humankind."

They are supreme examples of human courage in the face of impossible
odds.

THE TIMING

Most open resistance took place when the Jews finally realized that before them lay not more savage cruelty and slavery, but planned and pitiless extermination.

By mid-1942 in the ghettos, at least half the population had been deported. The death camps were an accepted fact; the remaining Jews knew they were doomed. By 1943 in the camps, the killing machinery had slowed down. The remaining Jews knew death was inevitable when they were no longer needed to keep the machinery running. In ghettos and camps, undergrounds began secretly organizing to revolt.

The same problems existed in both places. The underground received little or no aid from non-Jews outside; often members were betrayed by the very people they went to for help. Many were discovered and died under torture or were gassed before plans could be carried out. Yet patiently, with deepest secrecy, they managed to smuggle in a few weapons, which could take years to stockpile; they hid axes and knives, which sometimes they made for themselves.

When they fought with guns and ammunition, their bravery and cleverness always took the Nazis by surprise. As Goebbels confided to his diary: "One sees what the Jews can do when they are armed." When they had no arms, they fought with such things as sticks, boiling water, iron bars, acid, their bare hands.

However they fought, they took a toll among Germans far beyond their training and number.

THE WARSAW GHETTO

On September 5, 1942, the Nazis ordered all Jews in the Warsaw ghetto to report "for registration purposes," bringing with them food for two days. Once inhabited by more than 500,000, the ghetto now held approximately 115,000. They collected in a seven-square-block area that was roped off and surrounded by armed guards.

The Nazis' "two days" became one week. In that one week, more than 10,000 Jews a day were deported. Another 3,000 were shot. Forty-two thousand remained alive in the ghetto.

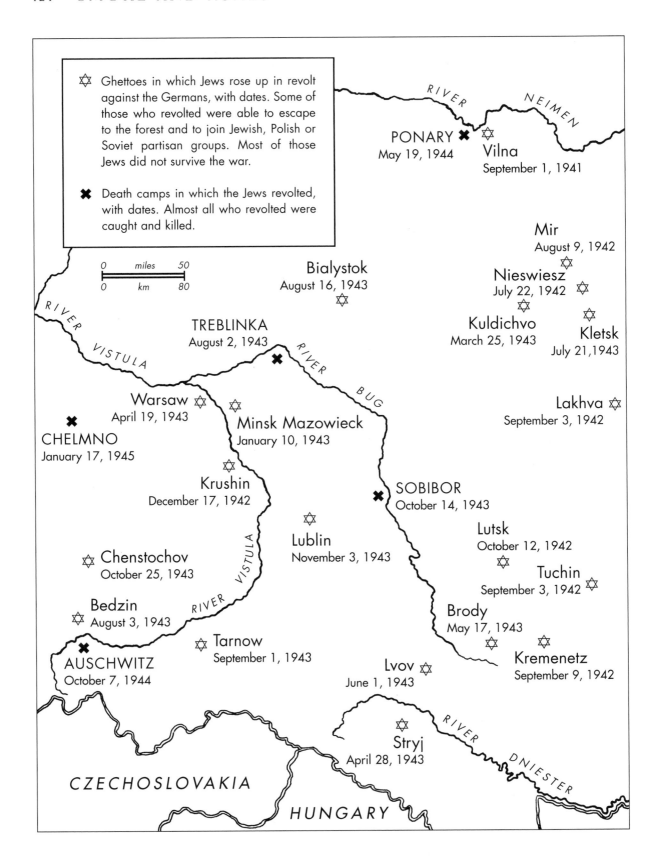

✡ Ghettoes in which Jews rose up in revolt against the Germans, with dates. Some of those who revolted were able to escape to the forest and to join Jewish, Polish or Soviet partisan groups. Most of those Jews did not survive the war.

✖ Death camps in which the Jews revolted, with dates. Almost all who revolted were caught and killed.

0   miles   50
0   km   80

RIVER   NEIMEN

PONARY ✖
May 19, 1944

Vilna ✡
September 1, 1941

Mir
August 9, 1942
✡

Nieswiesz
July 22, 1942 ✡

Kuldichvo
March 25, 1943
✡

Kletsk
July 21,1943
✡

Bialystok
August 16, 1943
✡

RIVER VISTULA

TREBLINKA
August 2, 1943
✖

RIVER BUG

Warsaw ✡
April 19, 1943

✡
Minsk Mazowieck
January 10, 1943

Lakhva ✡
September 3, 1942

✖
CHELMNO
January 17, 1945

✡
Krushin
December 17, 1942

RIVER VISTULA

✖ SOBIBOR
October 14, 1943

Lutsk
October 12, 1942
✡

✡
Lublin
November 3, 1943

Tuchin
September 3, 1942 ✡

✡ Chenstochov
October 25, 1943

Bedzin
✡ August 3, 1943

RIVER VISTULA

Brody
May 17, 1943
✡

✡
Kremenetz
September 9, 1942

✖
AUSCHWITZ
October 7, 1944

✡ Tarnow
September 1, 1943

Lvov ✡
June 1, 1943

RIVER DNIESTER

✡
Stryj
April 28, 1943

CZECHOSLOVAKIA

HUNGARY

The Jews called that teeming mass of tortured humanity "The Cauldron." It marked a turning point in the history of the ghetto, for it was then that the move to open resistance took on life. A ghetto leader wrote in his diary:

"The public wants the enemy to pay dearly. We shall attack him with knives, with sticks, with bullets. We will not allow him to stage a roundup, to seize people in the streets, because now everybody knows that every labor camp spells only death. We must resist. Young and old alike must oppose the enemy."

An underground already existed. Its members had belonged to Jewish youth organizations before the war. The two major groups were the Zionists, who believed in an eventual Jewish nation in Palestine, and the Bundists, who worked for Jewish freedom in a socialist Poland. Now all groups combined into the Jewish Combat Organization, called the ZOB from the abbreviation of its Polish name. Its members were young, in their early twenties or teens; their leader was twenty-three.

They were not trained in armed combat. "The merest German private knows more about organizing warfare than we do," a member said. But another had said simply, "We have nothing left but our honor—we can lose nothing else."

Not only did they lack training. They also had no weapons to speak of. When they asked the non-Jewish Polish underground—the Home Army—for help, they were given exactly ten revolvers. "I am not so sure," commented the army's commander, "that they will use the guns, anyhow."

At great peril, the most "Aryan"-looking young women and girls, some no older than children, went outside the wall. They bought weapons for huge sums from Italian soldiers, German deserters, from anyone money-hungry enough to sell them. The weapons were brought into the ghetto slowly, sometimes section by section.

The underground built bunkers—hidden places with no visible entrance. Behind stoves, under toilets, between walls, under basements and in attics, these rooms ranged in size from small spaces able to hold only a few people to large rooms that could hold dozens. Some were lightly equipped, others outfitted with heat, electricity, water, food, a radio, even a small library.

They constructed passageways that connected spaces within buildings, and between attic and basement bunkers in neighboring buildings; they dug tun-

nels between basements and courtyards. It became possible to move freely over a full city block without going outside.

They put sandbags at entrances and on windowsills. Sentry posts were established at corner apartments where the view of the street was the widest.

The Nazis tried several times to get Jews to report for deportation by making the usual promises. The ZOB distributed leaflets that exposed the lies one by one, and few Jews reported.

The Nazis began arrangements for the "resettlement" of factory workers and the removal of machinery. The night before the first deportation, the ZOB burned down a large factory with all its equipment. The next morning, only twenty-five workers appeared voluntarily.

The German authorities must have known by this time that the underground was at work. In fact, the leader of the Jewish Council had actually said to a Nazi officer, "I have no power. Another authority rules here." Yet the Germans did little to find the members or to stop their activities. Probably the explanation is an obvious one: they believed the Jews would collapse at the slightest pressure; they thought Jews would not fight. They were wrong.

Unexpectedly, on January 18, 1943, the ghetto was surrounded and SS troops marched in. They were met by ZOB gunfire. In the three days of fighting, the Nazis succeeded in rounding up far fewer Jews than usual. Fifty German soldiers were killed or wounded.

ZOB casualties were high. But the Germans had been forced to retreat.

The event electrified the ghetto. Thousands went into the bunkers, prepared to stay until forced out, ready to help the resistance in any way they could. The fighters were given food, clothing, all supplies but one—weapons.

The Polish underground, perhaps as surprised as the Germans, gave the ZOB another forty-nine revolvers, fifty grenades and some explosives. The resistance raised funds for additional supplies by taxing ghetto residents, even taking money from the Jewish Council.

The underground was in control; all energies went to planning the most effective means of fighting back. They organized into groups of ten, at least eight men and no more than two women; half or more were required to have their own weapons. There were just over one thousand of them.

SS Brigadier General Jürgen Stroop received the orders that came from Himmler: "The roundups in the Warsaw Ghetto must be carried out with relentless determination and in as ruthless a manner as possible. The tougher the attack, the better. Recent events show just how dangerous these Jews are." Stroop confidently expected the ghetto action to be over in three days.

Early in the morning of April 19, 1943, the ghetto was surrounded by SS men, German and Polish police, German army men, and Ukrainian volunteers. At 6:00 A.M., over two thousand heavily armed soldiers marched in, followed by guns and by tanks and trucks filled with ammunition. The Warsaw ghetto uprising began.

The Jewish fighters attacked. By 5:00 P.M., after eleven hours of fierce fighting, the Germans were forced out of the ghetto.

"We were happy and laughing," a fighter said. Jews hugged and kissed each other in the streets. A young woman remembered: "The rejoicing among Jewish fighters was great and, see the wonder and the miracle, those German heroes retreated, afraid and terrorized from the Jewish bombs and hand grenades, home made. . . . We the few with our poor arms drove the Germans away from the ghetto."

The Nazis brought in heavy artillery and tanks. The Jews fought back with revolvers, rifles, a few homemade mines and gasoline bombs. When they saw a tank burning, a fighter wrote: "We danced for joy. It was the happiest moment in our lives."

The Nazis delivered an ultimatum to the ZOB, demanding they lay down their arms. The Jews met them with gunfire and grenades instead.

The Nazis began setting fire to ghetto buildings. "One saw," Stroop wrote in his daily report, "that the Jews and bandits preferred to go back into the fire rather than fall into our hands." The ZOB answered by burning down the warehouse holding stolen Jewish property.

The Nazis brought in flamethrowers to force Jews out of the bunkers. "The only method," Stroop said, "to force this rabble and subhumanity to the surface." The ZOB rescued many of them.

"The Jewish quarter of Warsaw is no more."

The Nazis cut off gas, electricity and water to the ghetto. In defiance, the ZOB flew the forbidden red-and-white flag of Poland alongside the blue-and-white flag of the Jews.

On May 8, after three weeks of fighting, the Germans surrounded the headquarters of the ZOB. When those inside would not surrender, the Nazis sent in poison gas. Close to one hundred ZOB members, including their leader, committed suicide rather than be taken.

A few days later, about seventy-five Jews escaped through the filth of the sewers to the "Aryan" side of the city, where they planned to remain in hiding; some succeeded and lived out the war.

The fighting went on until May 16. By that time, most of the Jews had been killed, the rest deported to Treblinka. On Himmler's order the ghetto's major synagogue was blown up. The ghetto itself was razed to the ground. Stroop at last could write in his final report: "The Jewish quarter of Warsaw is no more!"

The Germans had brought in close to three thousand men and the most modern arms and weapons, including tanks, artillery and mines.

The Jews resisted them with about a thousand fighters, hand grenades, pistols, homemade bombs, one or two submachine guns and a few captured rifles.

These "inherently cowardly Jews," as Stroop called them, successfully fought the Nazis for a month. The Jewish "bandits and subhumans" had held off the Germans for almost as long as it took France to sign an armistice and for longer than it took all of Poland to surrender.

THE CAMPS

Treblinka. Treblinka, located fifty miles northeast of Warsaw, was one of the Operation Reinhard death camps, those built to exterminate the Jews of Poland. It was the second largest killing center after Auschwitz.

By 1943 Treblinka's work was nearly completed. The Jews of Poland were almost all dead, and shipments from elsewhere in Europe were slowing down. The sonderkommandos in the extermination area knew they would die when their work was done. Prisoners in the rest of the camp believed rightly that Treblinka would be demolished and themselves killed when the camp went out of operation.

The camp underground, numbering around a hundred young men, made careful plans for an uprising. A locksmith, called to repair the lock on the SS arsenal, made a wax impression of the lock and, over several months, a copy of the key was made. SS arms would be used to fight the SS.

The date was set: August 2, 1943, at 4:30 in the afternoon—light enough to see during the revolt, but close enough to nightfall to allow escapees the protection of the dark.

Before the hour, axes and wire cutters were smuggled from a toolshed to members of the underground. Using their key, several men went into the arsenal and passed twenty grenades, twenty rifles and several pistols to those waiting outside. The weapons were hidden under trash in a cart, and distribution began to other men strategically placed in the area.

The inmate whose daily job was to disinfect the buildings this day put smuggled gasoline into his tank and sprayed that instead. All was going according to plan.

Then the unexpected happened. An SS guard stopped and searched two of the men. He found forbidden money on their bodies, and began whipping them. At that, the SS man was shot.

The sound of the shot was taken as the signal to start the uprising—a half hour ahead of time, before all the details so carefully planned could be carried out. All the weapons had not yet been distributed, central control had not been established or other inmates informed, and the phone wires to the outside world had not been cut. But the decision to go ahead had to be made.

SS and Ukrainian guards were cut down by armed fighters. The buildings were set ablaze. But prisoners not directly involved in the uprising panicked. Some ran toward their blocks, as if for protection. Others stood helplessly in place and were shot where they stood. Hundreds ran to the first barbed-wire fence, cut openings and fled. In the 150 feet to the second fence, most were shot down by guards in the watchtowers. Many who made it that far were shot as they climbed; their bodies were a bridge for escapees behind them to scramble over and flee.

Those who lived ran to the forest—two hours away.

Approximately eight hundred joined in the uprising. Of these, almost one-half were killed inside the camp or near the fences. In the days of search and pursuit that followed, another three hundred were killed. Approximately one hundred prisoners, including most of the sonderkommandos, escaped the camp and made it to the forest.

No Nazi records of the uprising have been found. It is estimated that twenty Germans were killed or wounded, along with five or ten Ukrainian guards. Much of the camp had burned, though not the gas chambers; only about one hundred Jewish prisoners remained. The camp was dismantled by those Jews, who were then shot, during September and October 1943. All signs of the camp were removed or plowed under. A house was built, and a former Ukrainian camp guard was installed with his family to run the area as a working farm.

Sobibor. Sobibor was located about twenty-five miles east of the town of Chelmno. Like Treblinka, it was an Operation Reinhard death camp. Its assigned task was also nearly completed by 1943, and the work slowdown created the same fears in the Jewish inmates.

An uprising was planned. The date, October 14, 1943, the time, 3:30 in the afternoon. The plan: the sonderkommandos in the killing area would overcome the SS guards one by one with handmade hatchets and knives, take their guns and then march into the main camp at the usual time. The Jews there, arriving for roll call, would quickly be informed of events. Keeping in orderly lines to delay suspicion, they would march out through the main gate, the only area around the camp not planted with mines. Resistance members with their captured guns could shoot back at the Ukrainian guards in the watchtowers. The signal for the march to the gate was the cry of "Hurrah!"

On the date and time, the SS men were killed as they went into the death center's buildings, either on regular inspection or by being lured there. One SS officer could not be found, but delay was no longer possible. Now armed, the group marched into the main camp. Other prisoners began to assemble for roll call.

Suddenly a German came toward them. He was instantly killed. A group of women was approaching for roll call at just that moment. At the totally unexpected sight, one woman screamed and another fainted. The missing SS officer appeared and began shooting. Alerted watchtower guards aimed submachine guns at the prisoners. All hope of order was gone, but the quick decision was made to go ahead. As the leader of the revolt remembered it:

"'Comrades, forward!' I called out loudly.

"'Forward!' someone on my right repeated.

"'For our fatherland, forward!'

"The slogan reverberated like thunder in the death camp, and united Jews from Russia, Poland, Holland, France, Czechoslovakia and Germany. Six hundred pain-wracked, tormented people surged forward with a wild 'Hurrah!' to life and freedom. . . . "

But control had been lost. Prisoners began to run in all directions. The main gate was cut off by gunfire, and inmates broke through the barbed wire, to be killed by exploding mines. Others behind them used the dead bodies as markers for a safe path through the exploded mines, and ran across the field.

About three hundred broke out of the camp. One hundred were found and killed in the search that followed. Two hundred in the forest were not caught.

Estimates range from a few to over ten SS men and thirty-eight Ukrainian guards killed or wounded. Like Treblinka, in December 1943 Sobibor was dismantled. Here too all signs of the camp were removed and a working farm established to take its place.

Auschwitz. The non-Jewish underground in the Auschwitz main camp had made plans for an armed campwide revolt, in which the several hundred Jewish sonderkommandos in the Birkenau killing center would take part.

The sonderkommandos knew their lives were limited by their usefulness, just as those in Treblinka and Sobibor did. But each time they asked for the revolt to be scheduled, the non-Jewish underground told them the time was not yet ripe.

In 1944 their fears became fact. The gas chambers and crematoriums slowed down, and a group of three hundred sonderkommandos from Crematorium 4 was selected for "transfer." They knew that meant to their deaths. Yet, once again, the non-Jewish underground put them off, saying a revolt at that time would "be disastrous for the entire camp."

The sonderkommandos believed that the non-Jews hoped to stay alive until they were liberated by the Russian army, which all inmates knew was advancing toward them quickly. As Jews, the men in Birkenau had no such hope. The three hundred decided to stage a revolt alone. Their supplies: three pistols, a small amount of dynamite, insulated pliers and some hatchets and knives.

The day of the transfer, they made preparations to set Crematorium 4 on fire. When the three hundred were selected and made to stand aside, a hail of stones descended on the guards.

Fighting broke out. The prisoners attacked with their concealed hatchets and knives, and several SS men and Ukrainian guards went down. Crematorium 4 exploded.

The sonderkommandos in Crematorium 2 saw the smoke and thought the original planned general revolt had begun. They cut through the fence and fled.

About five hundred made it outside the barbed wire. All were caught and shot.

Four SS men were killed, several more wounded, and Crematorium 4 was destroyed.

On January 17, 1944, a little ahead of the advancing Russian army, most of the inmates of Auschwitz were evacuated to other camps. Those remaining behind, mostly Jews, were shot. Others overlooked by accident or too weak to move were left where they lay. On January 20, the Germans blew up the remaining crematoriums.

SUCCESSES OR FAILURES?

Almost all who revolted in Warsaw and other ghettos were killed, as were those in the camps. The camps did not stop functioning because of the rebellions that took place there; the Nazis had already made their own plans for that. The revolts may have hastened its happening, but just by a little; the war was almost over.

Only a small number of those who fled lasted longer than a brief while after their escape. Most were discovered, betrayed by informers, killed by anti-Semitic peasants, or else died in the forest. A few lived to join the partisans. Fewer still lived until the end of the war.

On these counts, the rebellions were failures. But on other counts they were not.

In the ghettos, fighting Jews took many German lives with them, more than this single chapter can show; in Warsaw, they kept several thousand desperately needed soldiers away from the front. In Treblinka and Sobibor, most of the inmates got out of the camp, a victory in itself. In Treblinka, over half who rebelled escaped a camp death; in Sobibor, over two-thirds.

They almost all died, yes. But they had torn that decision away from the hands of the Nazis. The Jews of the resistance died in a way they had freely chosen for themselves.

THE PARTISANS

Jews who escaped usually made their way to the surrounding countryside. But the forests offered no guarantee of safety. First, the city dwellers among them did not know how to live in the open. Second, if they were from a different country, they could not speak the language, had no useful connections among the people and did not know the area. Third, German patrols were always on the lookout for them. Last, and as usual, help could not be expected from the local populace. Out of fear or anti-Semitism, farmers and peasants usually would not aid them in any way. In Poland, members of the non-Jewish resistance often killed any Jews they found. Informers were everywhere; one pound of salt for one Jew was reward enough for many poor peasants.

Nevertheless, with courage, intelligence and luck, some Jews survived to become partisans. Many units began with escapees from particular ghettos—Lukov, Pulawy, Lublin, among others. The group that came to be called the Vilna Avengers originated with the underground members from that ghetto. The Kovno ghetto supplied the bulk of three partisan battalions.

They armed themselves as best they could, starting with whatever weapons they had taken with them. Occasionally they were supplied by peasants. They stole whenever possible. And of course they took the guns from German soldiers they ambushed.

Among the literally thousands of groups, several different kinds existed. Some were small, with fewer than five or ten men and women. Others were much larger. The Vilna unit finally numbered over four hundred; other groups grew to be close to a thousand. "Family camps," ranging in size from

Jewish partisan fighters from Vilna.

two to hundreds of families, were places of refuge for thousands of men, women and children. A family camp in Russia grew so large it was called "the Jewish city" and named Jerusalem.

About 5,000 Jews fought as partisans in central Poland; 4,000 were killed in the fighting. Forty-seven thousand Jews managed to escape to the forest in eastern Poland and western Russia; probably 15,000 lived long enough to become partisans, and most of these did not survive the war.

Little is known about Jewish partisans in most Russian areas occupied by the Nazis, because until this date little research has been allowed and almost no information been released. But there is enough evidence to show that there were large numbers of them.

From Lublin.

Exactly how many groups and individuals there were may never be known. What is known is that their number was not small and their revenge on the Nazis great.

As the war went on, partisan activity among Jews and non-Jews grew. The need for some kind of organization became clear. In addition, the non-Jewish resistance finally recognized Jewish fighting ability. Many partisan bands broke up into national groups—Lithuanian, Polish, Russian, Czech and so on—made up of Jews and non-Jews alike, all fighting their common enemy. Organized in this way, with some kind of central command for each and communication among them opened up, they were very much more effective in their battle against the Nazis. Some units, however, remained exclusively Jewish throughout the war.

From France.

Away from Eastern Europe—in France, Holland, Belgium and else-where—Jews in the resistance fought not so much as Jews but as citizens of their country. Even when a unit was a Jewish one, as with the Armée Juive in France, they fought because they were French for the sake of France, not only because they were Jews.

Partly because of this, the records of partisan activity in Western Europe rarely mention Jews as Jews. This much is known: they fought in greater numbers than their share in the general population. If they are not singled out as Jews, at the very least that is a sign that they shared the same courage and strength as the non-Jews who fought alongside them.

All over Nazi-dominated Europe, the Jewish partisans blew up bridges, sabotaged trains, destroyed German supplies, executed traitors, attacked patrols—the same things non-Jews did. Only, perhaps they fought with a greater fury and fire for revenge.

These men and women battled their enemy with barely enough arms, lit-tle enough food and shelter, and in constant terrible danger. As partisans, they had to hide their activities. As Jews, they had to hide their very existence.

Like most of the tortured and dying Jews they had left behind, they never believed the Nazis would win. Like them, they wanted to live to the end of the war, a time of peace and justice. They would have other things to do then, in honor of all those who had been murdered before them.

"If there is any purpose to our survival," a member of the resistance said, "then perhaps it is to give testimony. It is a debt we owe, not alone to the millions who were dragged to their deaths in crematoriums and gas chambers, but to all our fellow human beings who want to live in brotherhood—and who must find a way."

12

THE COMING END

I gave the order to burn out the abcesses of our . . .
inner well-poisoning and the foreign poisoning down
to the raw flesh.

                                           —Adolf Hitler

B<small>Y EARLY</small> 1943 N<small>AZI</small> G<small>ERMANY HAD LOST</small> several major battles in the war
against Russia. As the Germans retreated westward, the Soviet army
advanced steadily all along the eastern front. Each day brought the Russians
closer and closer to the camps and to the sites of the mass executions and
the bodies buried there.

As the defeat they knew was coming drew nearer, the Germans
increased their efforts to make Europe "Jew-free." At the same time they
attempted to get rid of any evidence of what they had done.

C<small>OMMANDO</small> 1005

In spring 1943 the Germans made the decision to dig up the corpses of
hundreds of thousands of those they had murdered, the greatest number by
far being the Jews, and then to burn them, leaving no traces behind.

SS Colonel Paul Blobel of Special Action Group C was selected to do
the job. The units in his charge were called Commando 1005. The action
was nicknamed *Spurverwischung*—Operation Blotout.

Blobel started at Chelmno. Jewish sonderkommandos opened up the
mass graves and burned the bodies on an elaborate pyre. These Jews were
then killed and burned with the rest. From there, Commando 1005 went to
Auschwitz, where Blobel instructed the camp commander, Rudolf Hoess, to
do the same with the bodies there—there were 107,000 of them. Then
Belzec, Sobibor and Treblinka. The last three accounted for over 500,000
bodies exhumed from their graves and burned.

Commando 1005 moved on to the sites of mass slaughter and burial in other parts of Eastern Europe. As before, Jewish sonderkommandos were brought to each site and ordered to dig up the bodies. They were commanded to extract any gold teeth remaining and to remove gold rings from fingers. "Every day," said one survivor of such a group, "we collected [over 17 pounds] of gold." A survivor who worked at execution sites in Lithuania recalled that between the end of September 1943 and April 1944, "We dug up altogether 68,000 corpses. I know this because two of the Jews in the pit . . . were ordered by the Germans to keep count of the bodies. . . ."

He went on: "Among those that I dug up I found my own brother. I found his identification papers on him."

The bodies were placed on pyres made up of crisscrossed logs or oil-soaked railroad ties placed over a deep pit. They were then burned, which could take several days. Blobel himself visited a huge ravine near Kiev called Babi Yar, where members of his Special Action Group and German Order

Paul Blobel. In charge of Commando 1005, Operation Blotout, and responsible for the deaths of over 30,000 Jews at Babi Yar in Ukraine.

Police had killed 35,000 Jews two years earlier. The burning pit there measured sixty yards long and was over eight feet deep.

Any remains were then obliterated by flamethrowers.

The emptied graves were disinfected, filled with soil, and grass was planted over them.

OPERATION HARVEST FESTIVAL

The uprisings in Treblinka and Sobibor surprised the Germans. They had never thought Jews capable of such action. And they were afraid that rumors of the uprisings would spread and revolts would happen elsewhere.

Auschwitz at the time of the uprisings was still operating efficiently; two or three trains holding as many as two thousand Jews each arrived daily, and the gassings there continued without stop. But aside from Auschwitz, there were still around 43,000 Jews in the General Government. Most were located in smaller slave-labor camps and in Maidanek. For the continued safe operation of Nazi plans, Himmler decided to annihilate all those Jews immediately. The operation was called *Erntefest* in German—Operation Harvest Festival.

To maintain secrecy and the element of surprise, it was decided that the operation would be carried out in all places at the same time. The date chosen: November 3, 1943.

That morning, several thousand police and SS men, divided among the camps, began their job. Music blared from loudspeakers to drown out the sound of the shots and screams. Between then and the evening of the same day, those approximately 43,000 Jews were murdered. It was the largest single massacre of Jews in the history of the Holocaust.

Operation Harvest Festival was the last and closing action of Operation Reinhard. The extermination of the Jews of Poland was considered a success.

THE DEATH MARCHES

The Germans had often moved large groups of prisoners hundreds of miles from one camp or another. Sometimes they went in open boxcars, sometimes on foot. Starvation, endless thirst, beatings, shootings, bitter cold or relentless heat took their toll each time.

But during the last six months of the war, when Germany's coming defeat was recognized by the most dedicated Nazi, these movements began on a scale never seen before. Hundreds of thousands of starved, emaciated prisoners marched across the frozen earth of wintertime Europe. Almost 60,000 were moved from Auschwitz, 25,000 from Stutthof, and unknown thousands from other camps including Dachau, Ravensbrück, Buchenwald, Neuengamme and Mauthausen. Those too weak to move were shot or left behind to die.

These thousands of prisoners were marched to camps closer to Germany, and eventually to camps inside Germany itself. The explanation:

Jews on a death march from Dachau. German civilians secretly photographed several of these marches.

Germany needed them to work. By this time, most were too weak or sick to work. Another explanation: to keep them from being found by the advancing Allies. But the bodies and the few alive left behind were enough evidence of the camps.

The marches made little sense to begin with. During the last month or so before Germany surrendered, they continued in a way that proved their senselessness. They became almost aimless wanderings, their destination sometimes unknown even to the soldiers guarding them. For example, the distance between one evacuated camp to another within Germany was 170 miles; the march traveled 215 miles. Two other camps were only 50 miles apart; the march took three weeks and covered 250 miles.

The last death march began when almost all of Germany was already occupied, and less than twenty-four hours before the surrender.

The Jews on these marches were clothed in rags, often barefoot, forced to sleep outside on bare ground or in unheated barns during bitter nights, not allowed to drink even at rivers, fed almost nothing if they were fed at all. In fact, if villagers offered the prisoners food, the prisoners were beaten or killed, not the villagers. "On the death march from Auschwitz," a survivor recalled, "German women heard we were prisoners and threw boiled potatoes. Those who picked up the potatoes died with a bullet—and a hot potato in their mouths."

The conditions on these marches do not need to be described. They were the continuation of the horrors of the camps. Their purpose was the same: the death of Jews. A German guard at a march said after the war:

"If I were asked whether the purpose of the march was . . . that the Jewish prisoners should gradually be driven to death . . . the manner in which [the march] was carried out speaks for it."

13

THE UNITED STATES AND GREAT BRITAIN

If horses were being slaughtered as are the Jews of
Poland, there would now be a loud demand for organ-
ized action against such cruelty to animals.
—Rabbi Meyer Berlin to
U.S. Senator Robert P. Wagner

In my opinion a disproportionate amount of time . . .
is wasted on dealing with these wailing Jews.
—A. R. Dew, British Foreign Office

Most of the world's free nations did little or nothing to aid the Jews
of Europe as they were being destroyed. They cannot claim ignorance,
because they knew all or most of the truth soon into the war if not before.
If they had chosen to act, from early on at the first signs in Germany to later
when the death camps were in full operation, they could have saved many
thousands and possibly millions of lives. But they did not.

There are exceptions to this, both among governments and people, and
they will be described in the next chapter. This chapter is devoted to a few
of the most important actions—and lack of actions—of the United States
and Great Britain.

THE FIRST YEARS

The anti-Jewish character of Hitler's government was known by all the
world and made plain by its actions soon after it came into power. The
Nuremberg Laws and the boycott of Jewish businesses received worldwide
publicity, almost all of it extremely critical of such "uncivilized" behavior. It
was during this period, from 1933 until the outbreak of war, that Jewish
emigration increased from Germany and Austria.

The European countries allowed Jews entry up to a certain point, as did the United States and Great Britain. No country, with two exceptions mentioned later, accepted them without serious restrictions.

The United States allowed only a certain number of people from each country to come to its shores. The quota for Germany was 25,957 a year. Yet from 1933 to 1938, it was never filled. In 1933, Hitler's first year in power, only 1,445 emigrated here from Germany. In 1937 the number permitted to enter reached only 11,536—and that was after the Nuremberg Laws, the boycott and the growing severity of anti-Semitism in Germany. The would-be immigrants were kept out perfectly legally.

American immigration law stated that a person could be refused a resident's visa if he or she was "likely to become a public charge" and therefore a financial burden. In order to live here, the immigrant had to prove he had enough money to support himself, or produce proof that his support was guaranteed by family or friends. This LPC clause, as it was called, was rarely enforced—possession of a hundred dollars was usually enough to allow entrance—until 1930, when unemployment was very high in this country. After then it was rigidly enforced.

This effectively kept the number of Jewish immigrants low. Generally poor, Jews from Eastern Europe were especially hard-hit. But even better-off Jews were gradually being driven to poverty by the Nazi schemes against them. They had been removed from most well-paying professions, their property and businesses were being taken from them, they had to pay several "taxes" when they left, and they were allowed to take very little money with them.

And unfortunately there is solid evidence that officials who made the decisions about who would be allowed a visa were applying the LPC clause more harshly than its framers had intended. Breckenridge Long, an assistant secretary of state, ordered overseas consulates to "put every obstacle in the way" of granting visas. Half of the available immigration slots for Europeans went unused.

The officials' actions reflected the reality of feeling in the United States. According to a survey in 1939, 83 percent of the American people wanted to keep the refugees out.

Economic reasons were set forth—such large numbers of immigrants would put Americans out of work—but the reasons are probably based on something less pleasant than that. Anti-Semitic feeling was high in America during the 1930s. This was partly because of the propaganda unleashed here by the Nazis and their sympathizers. But much of the propaganda fell on fertile soil.

The several anti-Semitic newspapers and magazines in the country had a good-sized readership, a hundred anti-Semitic organizations were active, and anti-Semitic radio programs were widely popular. Another survey found that the Jews were considered among the "least desirable" residents of America. In July 1939 over 30 percent thought that the Jews had "too much power," and 10 percent believed they should be deported.

Nonetheless, the number of people wanting to leave Germany, and then Austria, grew in number every year. It was truly an international problem. By 1938 the estimate was 660,000. Although officially it was called "the refugee problem," its Jewish character could not be denied; 300,000 were Jews, and 285,000 were Christians married to Jews. The remaining 75,000 were Catholics, fleeing Hitler's first—and unsuccessful—attempt to persecute the churches.

At the initiation of President Franklin Delano Roosevelt, an international conference was called to deal with the problem.

THE MEETING AT EVIAN

In July 1938 the representatives of thirty-two countries met at a luxury hotel in the French town of Evian on Lake Geneva. The United States said it would allow its full immigration quota to be filled from then on. The small countries of the Netherlands and Denmark, already burdened with refugees out of proportion to their sizes, said they would continue to allow them entry.

Aside from that, almost no changes in existing refugee policies were made. In one way or another, the countries at the conference echoed the words of the representative from Australia: "As we have no real racial problem, we are not desirous of importing one."

A group called the Intergovernmental Committee on Refugees was appointed, which had two primary aims. First, it would seek out places for the refugees to settle. Since almost all countries had already made known

Franklin Delano Roosevelt,
President of the United States,
1933–1945.

their unwillingness to
accept them, that aim
was doomed to failure.
Second, it would at-
tempt to negotiate with
Nazi Germany. The
committee called them
refugees; the Nazis right-
ly called them Jews. Negotiations about easing their plight, one can imagine,
would not have gotten very far.

No one took the committee very seriously. At its first meeting after the
Evian conference not all countries bothered to send a representative, and
those who came were of very low government rank.

After Kristallnacht on November 9, 1938, Roosevelt said, "I could scarcely believe that such things could occur in a twentieth-century civilization."
The United States withdrew its ambassador from Germany in protest. That
was all. No changes were made in the immigration laws at that time.

In 1940 and 1941, the American laws were made much more restrictive
by the addition of a strict security test. Each immigrant had to prove a clean
police record for the past five years. In other words, a Jew had to ask Nazi-
controlled police for proof of good behavior. Few did, or could.

Another obstacle stood in the way of immigrants from countries
opposed to the United States—which meant the nations overrun and controlled by the Nazis. If they had left close relatives behind, that was

Winston Churchill, Prime Minister of Great Britain, 1940–1945.

considered a security threat, a situation possibly harmful to America's interest and public safety. Such people were rarely granted permission to enter. Refugees from countries considered "unfriendly"—Germany and its allies—faced even greater hurdles to immigration.

The flow of immigrants fell to a trickle.

Then England helped to close things down. Palestine had been under British control since the end of the First World War in 1918 and was considered the Jewish National Home. Britain granted permits to Jews to live there, and some 550,000 had settled in Palestine. In 1939 England decided to limit immigration to Palestine to 75,000 at the rate of 10,000 a year; the surrounding Arab states would have to give approval for any change after that number was reached.

The meeting at Evian had influenced no one.

THE RIEGNER TELEGRAM

By September 1941 the war had reached all of Europe. In October Jews were forbidden to leave German-occupied territory. The Special Action

Groups moved through Eastern Europe, and Jews were gassed for the first time on December 8 in Chelmno. Their systematic murder had begun.

The Allies knew what was happening. Through 1941 and before, reports of mass murder had come to both the American and the British governments. Items appeared in the newspapers, but they were short, inconspicuous and placed far inside. The public was not concerned, neither were the governments.

In May 1942 a report came though from the Jewish Labor Bund in Poland. It traced the Nazi path through the country, region by region, month by month. It described the Special Action Groups, the mobile killing vans and the killing operation begun at Chelmno. It estimated that 700,000 had already been murdered, and concluded that the destruction of the Jews of Europe was the Nazis' purpose.

In England the public was informed and, along with the churches, spoke up in outrage. The government did nothing. In America only one newspaper—the *New York Herald Tribune*—gave the story accurate front-page prominence; Jewish organizations held protest rallies. The government did nothing.

In August 1942 a telegram was received by England and the United States. It was sent by Gerhardt Riegner, a refugee from Germany living in Switzerland and chief of the Geneva office of the World Jewish Congress. It said:

"Received alarming report that in Führer's headquarters plan discussed and under consideration, according to which all Jews in countries occupied or controlled by Germany numbering 3.5–4 million should, after deportation and concentration in the east, be exterminated. . . . The action planned for autumn; methods under discussion including prussic acid. . . . "

It was learned only in 1986 that the source of the information was a German anti-Nazi named Eduard Schulte. More about him appears in chapter 14.

The telegram arrived at the U.S. State Department and British Foreign Office. Riegner asked that a copy be sent to Rabbi Stephen Wise, America's most prominent Jewish leader, and to Member of Parliament Sidney Silverman in England. Silverman got the information. Rabbi Wise did not. The State Department not only stopped it, but a few months later they also asked the Geneva consulate not to forward news from such sources again.

Silverman sent a copy to Rabbi Wise. The State Department asked the rabbi not to publicize it until they could confirm its contents. They did so. In November, four months after the telegram was received, Rabbi Wise was permitted to hold a press conference.

The news was reported throughout the country, but once again not very conspicuously. The American public did not seem able to understand it as true, or possibly even to care. (As late as July 1944, with the war underway for three years and news of Nazi killings appearing in the press, 44 percent of Americans still believed Jews were a threat.)

The British public did respond, however. Perhaps because they were being bombed and felt the effects of war firsthand, they could accept the report as reality. Demands by members of Parliament, the clergy and other groups resulted in an English-sponsored international declaration denouncing the murder of Jews in the name of eleven Allied nations. It was released in Washington, London and Moscow.

They were talking to themselves. Nothing was done.

WHAT WERE THE REASONS?

There are at least five decent reasons why the Evian meeting accomplished nothing, and why the Bund report and Riegner telegram that came later also caused no action.

First, at the time of Evian in 1938, a worldwide depression was on. Unemployment was very high and the economies of most countries were not in very good condition. It is understandable that the entry of several thousand new residents would be considered a bad idea.

Second, the information about the Jewish mass murders that began to reach the West was just not believed. Nothing like such horror had occurred in the modern world, and it was simply beyond the ability of most people to grasp it as the truth. Even many Jews called the reports irresponsible.

Third, there was a basis in history for the disbelief as well. During World War I, stories of terrible German atrocities in Belgium had made headlines all over the world. German soldiers were accused of bayoneting babies and shooting helpless nuns. Those stories were false; they were circulated to whip up fighting spirit, particularly in America and England. The new, and now true, stories appeared little more than twenty years after the lies. People old enough to remember were not ready to believe atrocity stories again; they had been fooled once, and that was enough.

Fourth, the Arabs in Palestine and surrounding areas had revolted against the Jewish presence in 1936. The violence went on for two years, reaching a climax in 1938. Britain was afraid the Arabs would support the Nazis in the war it knew was coming. That is the major reason given for hardening immigration rules in 1939.

Fifth, World War II became global when the United States entered on December 7, 1941; England had been fighting since 1939. From then until 1943, the Allies were in serious danger of losing the war. Even when the mass-murder reports were believed, it was felt that little could be done because all energies had to be directed toward winning the war. Help for the Jews would have to take central place if it was to be successful. There was not enough Allied power, nor belief in victory, to allow that shift in armed strength.

And after 1943, when it was clear that the Germans were losing? What then? The officially given answer was: "The positive solution to this problem is the earliest possible victory over the Germans."

The only thing wrong with that, of course, was that at the rate the Nazis were killing them, there would be no Jews left in Europe at the end of the war.

THE BERMUDA CONFERENCE

Pressure on the British government from the public, clergy and Parliament was constant. To reduce some of the pressure, the British asked the Americans to hold a conference on the problem of finding places of refuge for victims of the Nazis. They wanted two restrictions. First, Palestine was not to be considered as a possibility. Second, the need for refuge would not be discussed as a problem of Jews. That might arouse criticism from other Allies, and in addition the possibility of "too many foreign Jews" being brought to England might arouse anti-Semitism at home.

The Americans agreed. Palestine would not be mentioned. The conference would not deal with Jews but with refugees in general—despite the fact that both countries knew that only all Jews were being exterminated, not any other people.

The delegates met in Bermuda on April 19, 1943 (the start of the Warsaw ghetto uprising, though they did not know it). Among the Americans was a member of the State Department who had tried to stifle all news of the extermination. Another believed that Hitler himself was really behind American-Jewish pressure for action.

Several paragraphs could be spent describing this conference. But since from the very beginning the purpose was to lessen some of the public disapproval of both governments, it would be wasted space to do so. The report issued after the conference made it so obvious little was done that it was kept secret for as long as possible. In the end, the conference was responsible for saving 630 refugees at a camp set up one year later in North Africa.

Other than that, nothing was done.

THE OFFERS OF ROMANIA AND BULGARIA

Romania and Bulgaria were allies of Germany, not conquered nations. They kept a certain amount of independence. Jews faced at least some of the usual restrictions in both countries, and each had involved itself in the Final Solution to some degree. But when the tide of the war turned against Germany, both wanted a little Allied sympathy when the war was over.

On February 13, 1943, Romania offered to cooperate in the removal of 70,000 Jews to a place chosen by the Allies, suggesting Palestine as the best. It asked about $130 per Jew, more to be decided upon if Romanian ships were used. At about the same time, Bulgaria decided to separate itself from the Final Solution; the government had begun carrying it out, but it had never been popular with the Bulgarian churches or people. Bulgaria offered to allow 30,000 Jews to leave.

The American State Department's response to the Romanian offer was that it was "without foundation" and that it probably came from the German propaganda machine, meant to "create confusion and doubt within the United Nations." The reaction to the Bulgarians was not much different. Britain's response was more blunt. The foreign minister is remembered as saying, "If we do that, then Jews will want us to take similar steps in Poland

and Germany. There simply are not enough ships and means of transportation in the world to handle them."

The reason, expressed again and again, was much more basic. There was no place to put them. The British had already noted that they were "concerned with the difficulties of disposing of any considerable number of Jews should they be rescued from enemy-occupied territory." Now the government said it would not follow up these possible means of escape at least partly because it would "lead to an offer to unload an even greater number on our hands."

A spokesman for the U.S. State Department's Division of European Affairs wrote that to take up the offer was "likely to bring about new pressure for an asylum in the Western Hemisphere." He added, "So far as I know we are not ready to tackle the whole Jewish problem." A State Department official commented that the rescue proposals would "take the burden and the curse off Hitler."

Nothing was done.

THE BOMBING OF AUSCHWITZ

On April 10, 1944, two young Slovakian Jews escaped from Auschwitz. They reached the Jewish Slovakian underground and dictated a thirty-page report. They spared no details about the purpose of Auschwitz and how it functioned. They described the gas chambers that held "2,000 people" each, the "SS men with gas masks" who dropped in the poison, and the removal and burning of the bodies.

By mid-June the information had reached Switzerland and the Allies. England and America had known about the existence of Auschwitz before, but not its purpose. Now they knew it was a killing center for Jews. News of it began to appear in the press, and by late June the truth about Auschwitz was known everywhere.

The report appeared at about the same time as the start of the mass deportation of Hungarian Jews to the camp. The Czech underground and several Jewish groups asked the Allies to bomb at least the railway lines leading to Auschwitz from Hungary. It was understood that this might not stop the mass killings, but at least it would slow them down enough to save thousands of lives.

Germany by this time was unmistakably losing the war. Heavy Allied bombing had already burned several of its cities to the ground.

American planes had dropped bombs near Auschwitz on over ten different occasions in a period of six months. The synthetic rubber factories of I. G. Farben had been bombed, and they were only five miles away from Birkenau. Amazingly, Auschwitz I and Birkenau had already been bombed—by accident. More damage had been done by those few bombs—with greater damage to SS buildings and men—than had been done deliberately in the bombing of the factories, which were only slightly damaged.

The British response to the request was firm: "We have no option but to refrain from pursuing the proposal in present circumstances." The "present circumstances" were "the very great technical difficulties involved."

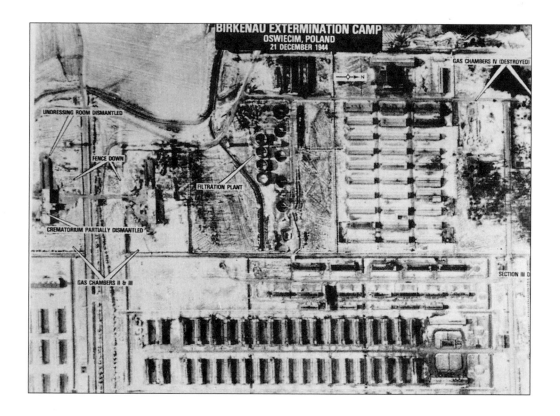

Auschwitz and Birkenau were photographed by Allied planes. This photograph was taken in December 1944. The labels were added after the war. Oswiecim is the Polish name, which the Germans changed to Auschwitz.

*Assistant Secretary of War
1941–1945, John J. McCloy.*

It should be repeated. Over ten bombing raids occurred near the killing camp. Factories five miles away from the gas chambers had already been accidentally bombed on the same raid. Furthermore, other planes had flown over the camp at least twice to take photographs. The Allies knew what Birkenau looked like.

What "great technical difficulties"?

Further, if the Royal Air Force were to be used, "valuable lives would be lost." What were Jewish lives, then?

In America the request went to John J. McCloy, assistant secretary of war. Here was his response:

"After a study it became apparent that such an operation could be executed only by diversion of considerable air support essential to the success of our forces now engaged in decisive operations elsewhere . . ."

But such a diversion or shift had already been made to within five miles, and accidentally to the death camp itself.

"[Such bombing] would in any case be of such doubtful efficacy that it would not warrant the use of our resources."

It would have saved thousands of Jewish lives by temporarily slowing things down. That is no "doubtful efficacy."

He said more.

"There has been considerable opinion to the effect that such an effort, even if practicable, might provoke even more vindictive action by the Germans."

More vindictive—more terrible, bloodthirsty and cruel—than Auschwitz?

Nothing was done.

THE BRITISH SECRET INTELLIGENCE SERVICE (SIS)

In a building on an English estate north of London called Bletchley Park, a group of men and women set out to break German codes. They were part of England's Secret Intelligence Service (SIS). Their successes were many and hard-won; there is no question that their accomplishments helped shorten the war, posssibly by as much as two years.

Richard Breitman's *Official Secrets: What the Nazis Planned, What the British and Americans Knew* deserves mention here as the source of most of the information that follows.

From 1939 until the end of the war, the Bletchley Park group could read many radio communications to and from the German army and SS high command, soldiers in the field and the Order Police. These messages included information on German military plans and other situations. They also included messages from the Order Police and some from the SS about killing actions in Poland and then in the Soviet Union. The largest number were against Jews.

In September 1941 the service wrote to Prime Minister Winston Churchill: "The fact that the Police are killing all Jews that fall into their hands should by now be sufficiently well appreciated. It is not therefore proposed to report these butcheries specially."

As the war progressed, the SIS learned more and more of the extent of the slaughter. The SS code was extremely difficult, but even there the service had some success. For much of the war, the Order Police sent their messages in a code the SIS deciphered easily. The Bletchley Park Group knew where and how masses of Jews were being murdered.

As Breitman noted, "If there had been any Allied disposition to interfere with Nazi killing operations or to undertake or arrange rescue efforts, [the] police decodes and the SS decodes would have provided essential details about location and activities. . . . But there was no move in that direction."

Some distrust existed between the British and American secret services. For that and other reasons, the SIS kept to itself much of what it knew of the ongoing slaughter. In particular, almost all decodes from the Order Police were filed as "Most Secret" and "To Be Kept Under Lock and Key: Never to Be Removed From Office!" There are two possible explanations.

First, in the early years of the war, the persecution of Jews could be seen as terrible, but not as a major part of the Germans' overall management of the conflict. The wholesale murder that was to come could not be foreseen or imagined.

Second, the SIS believed that an accidental leak or some British action would alert the Germans to the fact that the codes had been broken.

The two explanations for wartime secrecy may or may not sound convincing. They may or may not be the complete truth.

Yet the British did not release crucial information even after the war.

The Order Police and its involvement in the systematic murder of the Jews is described in chapter 4. The participation of these men was almost as great as that of the SS; the Holocaust could not have come so close to making Europe "cleansed of Jews" without their participation.

British intelligence knew about the role of the Order Police. They did not reveal this information at any time during the war.

Neither did they reveal it after the war.

Because of that, the Order Police was not classified a criminal organization on the level of the SS, Gestapo and the Nazi Party. The chief of the Order Police, Kurt Daleuge, was not judged important enough to be considered a major war criminal. He was executed by the Czechs in 1946 for an unrelated reason.

Why did the British Secret Intelligence Service keep much of its early knowledge of the murder of Europe's Jews secret? Why was the crucial information about the role of the Order Police kept hidden even after the war? What else did they learn that remains "Never to Be Removed From Office!"?

The British have yet to answer.

A LATE EXCEPTION: THE WAR REFUGEE BOARD

On January 13, 1944, the American secretary of the treasury received a confidential report prepared by a Treasury Department lawyer that said in part:

"One of the greatest crimes in history, the slaughter of the Jewish people in Europe, is continuing unabated. . . .

"I am convinced on the basis of the information which is available to me that certain officials in our State Department . . . have been guilty of not only gross procrastination and willful failure to act, but even of willful attempts to prevent action from being taken to rescue Jews from Hitler."

He went on to give examples that proved beyond all doubt that the State Department attempted to hamper rescue attempts and to cover up or delay information about the Final Solution.

The report was passed on to the president.

On January 22, 1944, President Franklin Delano Roosevelt signed Executive Order 9417, and the War Refugee Board, or WRB, was born. The WRB was set up "for the rescue, transportation, maintenance and relief of the victims of every oppression." It mentioned in particular that it would attempt to slow down the "Nazi plans to exterminate all Jews."

A representative of the WRB in Turkey met with a high Romanian government official and told him Romania would be held responsible for the 48,000 Jews in camps inside its territory. With the promise of American visas for the official and his family, it was agreed to evacuate the camps. With the demand to withdraw the anti-Jewish laws in effect, the same tactic was used on Bulgaria. Helped along by considerable public and church opposition to those laws, they were withdrawn.

In Hungary the WRB helped fund the rescue work of Raoul Wallenberg, the Swedish diplomat who saved 100,000 Jewish lives. The board worked with and helped fund underground organizations all over Europe.

Against the wishes of the State Department and the British Foreign Office, and at the insistence of the WRB, President Roosevelt issued a statement that was printed and radioed all over Europe—dropped as leaflets from planes, read in foreign-language broadcasts and printed by underground newspapers. It was one of the rare times that the Jews were mentioned as particular victims of the Nazis. Part of the statement said:

"In one of the blackest crimes in all history—begun by the Nazis in a day of peace and multiplied a hundred times since the war—the wholesale systematic murder of the Jews of Europe goes on unabated at every hour. . . .

"None who participate in these acts of savagery shall go unpunished. . . . All who share the guilt shall share the punishment."

The message may have helped push Romania and Bulgaria into action. There is no question that it boosted the morale of the conquered peoples. It may have given some of the imprisoned Jews the extra strength they needed to live until liberation.

In these ways and others, the WRB succeeded in saving the lives of over 200,000 Jews, and 20,000 non-Jews as well. This was accomplished in the several short months of its existence.

It is almost painful to think what the board might have done if it had been given enough money, which it was not; if it had had the support of the State Department, which it did not; if it did not have to fight British disapproval and opposition, which it did; and if it could have begun its work before the Final Solution was on its way to completion.

A POSSIBLE CONCLUSION

Much has been left out of this chapter, including the attempts of people in government and elsewhere to change attitudes and help the dying Jews. But since the result was always the same—little was done—only the most important points and responses seemed necessary to mention. They show what government records reveal to be the overall attitude and reaction.

Perhaps the hideous enormity of the massacre could not be understood at first. Then it became clear that no one knew what to do with these Jews. It is also clear that some unspoken anti-Semitism lay at the bottom of much of what happened. That picture comes clearer with one simple question: If these had been one million—two million—six million Protestants or Catholics, then what would have been done?

14

THE RESCUERS AND THE RIGHTEOUS

I think you have a responsibility to yourself to behave decently.

—Marion P. Pritchard, who helped
save 150 Dutch Jews

Yet there were those who did help. Sometimes the help consisted of food left by the roadside as Jews on death marches passed by, sometimes of safe hiding places in barn lofts, pigsties, under floorboards. Children left with Polish families were taught how to act like Catholics; monasteries and nunneries took in whole families. Officials illegally supplied passports, visas or false papers. Governments refused to obey or found ways to weaken Nazi demands.

The number of rescuers and helpers is not large. The courage it required was immeasurable. They and their families faced a concentration camp at best, death at worst. Officials risked jobs and careers. Germans who helped chanced death and disgrace for their families. Governments faced a complete Nazi takeover.

The identities of many, indeed most, are unknown. The thousands who hid Jews in Nazi Berlin, in "Aryan" Warsaw and other cities, the peasants and farmers who fed and nursed escapees from the pits or camps—they may remain anonymous forever. Their reward lies in the memories of those Jews they helped to keep on living when the whole world seemed to want them to die.

Here are a few of the people and governments who had the courage to care and the daring to act.

TO CARE AND TO ACT

Elizabeth Abegg. Abegg's home in Berlin, the capital of Germany, was a place of rescue and help for Jews right under the noses of the Gestapo. She fed them, gave them money, often gained by selling her own possessions, got

Jewish children were sheltered by Christian families and raised as Catholics to escape detection. The x marks the Jewish altar boy outside a Catholic church in Poland.

them ration cards and visas and found them safe places in and out of the country. A former teacher, she organized a network among her pupils and friends that is believed to have saved at least 80 Jews, among them 24 children.

Petras Baublis. In charge of a home for infants in Kovno, Lithuania, Baublis offered to smuggle Jewish children out of the ghetto and hide them in the home. From priests who were friends, he obtained blank birth certificates that he made them agree to sign, stating that this was a Christian child. He is believed to have saved at least nine Jewish children.

Bulgaria. Bulgaria was an ally of Germany. Bulgarian Jews were rather well integrated into the society, and the anti-Jewish legislation was not as severe as in other Nazi-controlled countries. But eventually a pro-Nazi interior minister agreed to deportation to the camps and plans were drawn up. The

Jews in Bulgaria's newly acquired territories of Thrace and Macedonia were destroyed. But the Jews of "Old Bulgaria" were not deported. The government refused, and king, church and people protested. In response to intense German pressure, Jews were then sent to live in small country towns, but eventually this restriction was lifted and all anti-Jewish legislation canceled. Bulgaria's fifty thousand Jews survived.

Le Chambon-sur-Lignon. In this tiny mountain village in south-central France, Pastor André Trocmé and his wife, Magda, gave refuge to fleeing Jews. The villagers followed their example and took Jewish adults and children into their homes. When danger of discovery by the Germans grew acute, farmers brought the refugees into the countryside and, sharing simple homes and short rations, kept them there until it was safe to return. Asked for a list of Jews in the village, Pastor Trocmé refused and was arrested. On his release, he continued helping Jews, as did all the residents of Le Chambon. The villagers saved the lives of five thousand Jews.

Denmark. Because they were Scandinavians, the Danes were considered "Aryans" by the Nazis. After their defeat by the Germans in April 1940, they were permitted to keep their own government and were largely left alone. There was no anti-Jewish legislation until the fall of 1942, when Hitler changed his mind and sent an SS officer to represent German authority. The resulting increased oppression provoked incidents of resistance, which brought the German army into the country as occupiers for the first time. Alerted to the coming deportation of their Jews, almost all the citizens of this tiny country contributed whatever they could—money, food, shelter, boats large and small—to get them ferried across to Sweden and to safety. Four hundred Jews were caught and sent to a concentration camp, which they survived because of great pressure from the Danish government. All eight thousand Danish Jews made it safely through the war, except for fifty-one who died in the camp of natural causes, and thirty who drowned while fleeing to Sweden.

Georg Ferdinand Duckwitz. Duckwitz was a naval attaché in the German legation in Copenhagen, Denmark. From 1939 on, he passed secret information to the Danish resistance. He alerted the underground and the neutral Swedish government that the boats coming into port were for the purpose of deporting Jews, thus giving them time to mount the scheme that succeeded in saving all but a few of the Jews of Denmark. Asked why he put himself in such danger, he replied: "I did not think my life was more important than the lives of eight thousand Jews."

Finland. Finland joined Germany in attacking the Soviet Union. It was used as a base of operations thereafter but never occupied. Asked by Himmler to deport its Jews, the Finnish minister refused to consider it. The Germans captured eight, only one of whom survived. All but seven of Finland's two thousand Jews survived the war.

Herman Graebe. Graebe worked as a civilian employee for the German Railways during the war. He joined the Nazi party in 1931 but later renounced his membership. Assigned to Ukraine, he hired and protected hundreds of Jews, providing them with food and medical care, transit visas and false papers. In a confrontation with an SS officer, he saved one hundred Jews about to be deported. Graebe was the only German civilian witness for the prosecution during the Nuremberg Trials after the war. Shunned by his countrymen at war's end, he left Germany and settled in the United States.

Paul Grueniger. Grueniger was a police commander in St. Gallen, Switzerland, when the government closed its borders with Austria to all refugees. He found safe entry points for thousands to cross illegally. Brought to trial for disobeying orders, he was found guilty and dismissed. Grueniger earned a bare living as a substitute teacher until his death in 1972. In 1995, in the same court where he had been condemned 55 years earlier, Paul Grueniger was officially pardoned and rehabilitated by the Swiss government.

Dr. Adelaide Hautval. Hautval was a French doctor who protested the treatment of Jews and was eventually sent to Auschwitz. She was the inmate doctor in the women's section of the infamous Block 10, where medical experiments were performed. When a typhoid epidemic broke out, which meant immediate selection for the gas, she did not report it and hid the most obviously sick, thus saving their lives. She refused to participate in any of the experiments in any way. When asked by a chief SS doctor if she saw any difference between herself and the Jewish prisoners, she answered, "I have indeed perceived people different than myself—and you are one of them." Brave, unbelievably compassionate, she was called "The Angel in White" and "The Saint." She used to say to those around her, "Here we are all condemned to death. Let us behave like human beings as long as we are alive." She returned to France at the end of the war.

Italy. Italy was a major ally of Germany. Jews had lived in Italy since 200 B.C. and, by the twentieth century, were permitted full participation in all elements of life. Nazi pressure brought anti-Jewish legislation in 1938, but little was done to enforce the laws. The Italians did not respond to deportation demands. Jews remained safe until the government fell and Germany occupied the country. The Italian army, forced to take part in the roundups, kept Jews as comfortable as possible and helped many to escape the country or to go into hiding. Endangered Jews were hidden in nunneries and monasteries; nuns with printing presses ran off false papers by the thousands. The Italians are credited with saving all but 7,500 of their over 40,000 Jews.

Josef and Stephania Macugowski. The Macugowskis lived in the small Polish town of Nowy Korczyn. The Radza family—Miriam, six; Zahave, nine; Sarah, ten; and their parents—lived in a cramped space under the floorboards in the Macugowskis' kitchen for two and a half years, along with four other Jews. The Macugowskis convinced the Germans to let them stay on as caretakers when their house was taken, thus saving the Jews from discovery. Meeting again over forty years later in New York, the Radza daughters said, "You are our adopted parents." Josef Macugowski replied, "You are my daughters."

Norway and Sweden. Sweden was a neutral country; it fought on no one's side and remained free. After the deportation of Norwegian Jews began, the Swedish minister in Berlin declared his government's willingness to accept the Jews remaining in Norway. When this was rejected, the Swedish government then offered Swedish citizenship to all Jews who had once been

Norwegian citizens; as Swedes, they would be safe. It then invited arrested Jews to become citizens. With the help of the Norwegian resistance, more than half of Norway's Jews made it to Sweden and to safety. Sweden also backed Raoul Wallenberg's activities in Hungary and provided haven for the Danish Jews.

Marion P. Pritchard. Pritchard was a student in Amsterdam during the German occupation of Holland. In the first two years, as restrictions against Jews increased, she helped find extra or false ration cards for those without money and helped some to hide. When deportations began and the Nazi purpose became clear, she made arrangements to hide Jews wherever she found a willing helper or usable space. Three times—twice within five months—she registered a newborn Jewish baby as her own so records would show it to be a gentile. Arrested by the Gestapo for six months and tortured, she revealed no secrets. She lived outside Amsterdam for the last two years of the war, caring for a Jewish man and his three children. Pritchard participated in saving the lives of 150 Jews. She is now a practicing psychoanalyst in Vermont.

Angelo Roncalli. Bishop Roncalli represented the Vatican in Turkey when Hungarian deportations were at their height in 1944. He sent thousands of baptismal certificates to Budapest. Since converts to Catholicism were not treated as Jews in Hungary, these proofs of conversion would save lives. Shortly thereafter, thousands of Jews, from the most religious to the least, were "baptized" in mass ceremonies held in Budapest's air raid shelters and thus saved from deportation. Roncalli's position was unlike that of his pope, Pius XII, who refused to intervene directly in any rescue work. The Bishop had said to a representative from the War Refugee Board: "I am always ready to help you in your charitable work so far as is in my power and as far as circumstances permit." Roncalli later became Pope John XXIII.

Oskar Schindler. Schindler, an ethnic German businessman living in Czechoslovakia, took over an enamelware firm in Poland and made a fortune filling orders for the German army. Through bribery and charm, he arranged to keep 500 workers from the Cracow ghetto safe in his factory during roundups and deportations. Eventually he built housing for them and

*Marion Pritchard during the time
she helped save 150 Dutch Jews.*

*Pope John XXIII. As Bishop Angelo
Roncalli in 1944, he was responsible for
saving thousands of Hungarian Jews.*

Oskar Schindler.

acquired extra food and medical care, all paid for out of his own pocket. In 1944 Schindler went back home, taking his workers with him, and operated an armaments factory. He requested an additional 700 male Jewish workers and got them, but by some mix-up their wives, daughters and mothers were shipped to Auschwitz. He managed to get the 300 women out—the only known example of such an accomplishment—and brought them all back together again. He is responsible for saving 1,200 Jewish lives. He said, "I did what I could, what I had to do, what my conscience told me I must do. That's all there is to it. Really, nothing more."

Eduard Schulte. Schulte was the chief executive officer of a family-owned industrial firm in Germany employing 30,000 workers. His contacts among high-ranking Nazis were many. While in Zurich, Switzerland, on business, he began passing information to the Allies about German war plans. He was the source of the information in the Riegner telegram that alerted the Western Allies to the planned extermination of the Jews. Reported to the SS by a Swiss typist, he was warned in time to flee from his home in Germany to Switzerland, a neutral country, where he lived out the rest of his life. After

Aristedes de Sousa Mendes.

the war, his family was denied payment from the West German government for the loss of their family business; in passing information to the Allies, the Federal Republic said he had committed a crime "punishable according to the law of every country." His identity as the source of the Riegner telegram's information became known only in recent years.

Anton Schmid. Born in Austria and drafted into the German army, Anton Schmid was stationed in Vilna, Lithuania, in 1941. He witnessed Jews being herded into ghettos and thousands shot, and wrote to his wife that he "had to help them." Schmid managed to hide over 250 Jews and supplied the Jewish underground with arms and forged papers. He was caught and executed in April 1942. In his last letter Schmid said, "I merely behaved as a human being."

Aristedes de Sousa Mendes. De Sousa Mendes was Portuguese consul in Bordeaux, France, in 1940. His government had refused visas to any of the thousands of refugees escaping the German advance. After turning his house into a refuge, de Sousa Mendes gave all who asked a visa into Portugal and the path to freedom. Recalled home for acting against orders, he passed through Bayonne, France, found the same situation there and once again distributed

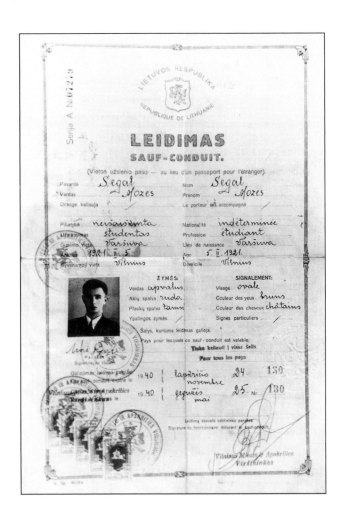

Visa to Japan issued in 1940 by Sempo Sugihara, Japanese consul in Lithuania, to Mozes Segal, then eighteen years old. It saw him safely through Russia and then to Japan. Eventually he emigrated to the United States. In his later years he became a professor of economics at Dartmouth College.

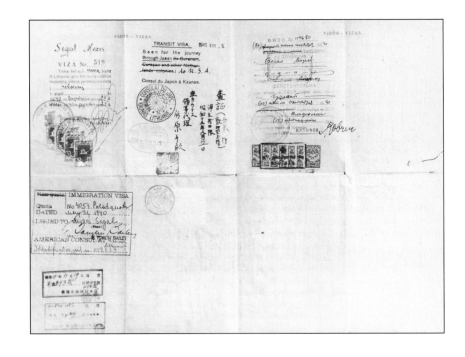

visas. The border to Spain was closed at Hendeye, where the Spanish government had expected the refugees to cross on their way to Portugal. Discovering this, de Sousa Mendes brought a group to a border station so small it had not yet received the orders and identified himself as the Portuguese consul; the refugees were allowed through. De Sousa Mendes is believed to have saved some 30,000 from the Nazis, at least 10,000 of whom were Jews. He lost his position and career, and finally came to the United States. Not honored by his country until 1998, he had said, "I cannot but act as a Christian."

Sempo Sugihara.

Sempo Sugihara. Sugihara was Japanese consul general in Kovno, Lithuania, from 1939 to 1940. When war broke out, his office was flooded with requests for safe-conduct visas to Japan from Jews in Lithuania and from German-occupied Poland. Disobeying his government, he issued visas to all who came to him. Transferred to Berlin partly as punishment, he tossed stamped visas from the window of his train to the desperate Jews on the platform. Sugihara saved the lives of over 3,000 Jews. He said: "I cannot allow these people to die. . . . Whatever punishment may be imposed on me, I know I should follow my conscience." After the war Sugihara was dismissed from the diplomatic service and spent the remainder of his life in disgrace working at menial jobs.

A few of the Jewish children saved by the village of Le Chambon-sur-Lignon. With them is Dr. Juliette Usach, who sheltered several.

Selahattin Ulkumen. Ulkumen was Turkish consul general on the Nazi-occupied island of Rhodes in 1944. He intervened to save over 200 Jews from deportation to death camps. In retaliation, the Germans bombed his official residence, killing his wife, who was then nine months pregnant. The 1,500 Jews remaining died in Auschwitz. The 200 Ulkumen saved were the only Rhodes Jews to survive the Holocaust.

Raoul Wallenberg. Wallenberg was a successful Swedish businessman sent to Hungary in July 1944, after more than one-third of the Jews there had already been deported. His mission was to save as many of the remainder as possible. He did so by designing impressive-looking "protective passes" accepted by both Germans and Hungarians as signs of official connection with neutral Sweden. He printed thousands of these meaningless papers and gave them to Jews in danger wherever he found them—on the streets, in deportation trains, on death marches—and whenever he was asked. He acquired some thirty houses in which Jews lived, the Swedish flag over the front door ensuring their safety. Soon representatives of other neutral nations in Budapest followed suit, the resulting collection of Jewish safe houses called "the international ghetto." A total of 120,000 Hungarian Jews survived the war. Wallenberg is credited with saving 100,000 of them.

Wallenberg was taken into custody by the Russians on January 17, 1945, and vanished from sight. The Russians lied or denied knowledge of his

Raoul Wallenberg.

condition or whereabouts. Not until November 2000 did they admit he had been executed in 1947. The reason for his death is unknown.

In the Eye of the Storm

A dictatorship as complete as Nazi Germany had rarely existed in the world. It took little more than a bad joke about Hitler or a pessimistic comment about the outcome of the war to result in a beating or a jail sentence, sometimes worse. If an act was considered treason, the accused went to trial before a so-called People's Court. As with everything Nazi, the People's Court offered no justice. It was a platform for vicious sarcasm, speeches and dramatics for the fanatic Nazi audiences that attended such trials. Defense lawyers could not defend the accused; they put themselves in danger if they spoke up too well for those already judged guilty of crimes "against the German folk and nation."

Imagine, then, what it must have taken for any meaningful resistance against the regime to exist. For there was resistance to the Nazis in Germany, as hard as that may be to believe. It was not well organized and was rarely successful for more than a short time, but it existed. Three of the examples that follow are among the most well known and justly famous; the fourth is less well known but deserves an equally important place.

Dietrich Bonhoeffer. Bonhoeffer was a Protestant pastor and theologian. He believed that Christianity could not coexist with Nazism and insisted that

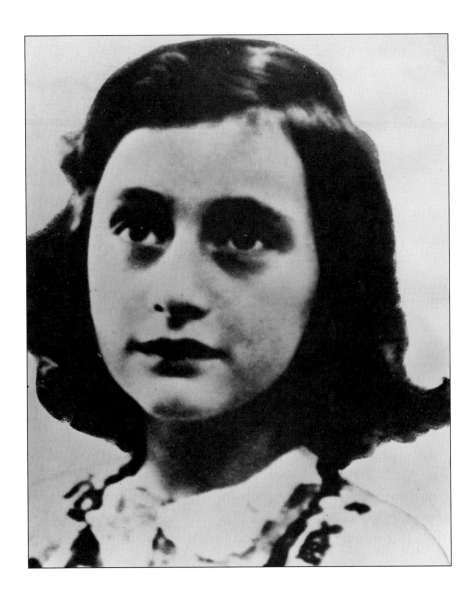

Anne Frank and her family went into hiding at the Nazi takeover of Holland. Hidden away in airless, dim rooms, they were cared for by Miep Gies and her husband Jan from July 1942 until they were betrayed and deported in August 1944. Only Otto Frank, Anne's father, survived.

Anne kept a diary during her time in hiding, which the Germans tossed aside as trash. Now a famous book that has sold millions of copies all over the world, Anne Frank: The Diary of a Young Girl *is Anne's life in her own words as she was growing up in a terrible time.* "In spite of everything I still believe that people are good at heart," *she wrote.* "I can feel the sufferings of millions and yet, if I look up at the heavens I think that it will all come out right and that peace and tranquility will return again."

Anne Frank died of typhus in Bergen-Belsen in March 1945. She was fifteen years old.

the church had the duty to aid all victims of the regime whether Christian or not. Bonhoeffer helped Jews escape and was long active in the resistance. Known to have contact with many involved in the July 20th Plot to assassinate Hitler, he was arrested by the Gestapo and sent to a concentration camp, where he was executed on April 9, 1945.

July 20th Plot. On July 20, 1944, a bomb in a briefcase was left under the table in a room where Hitler and some of his military men were having a conference. The bomb exploded, but Hitler received only minor injuries and no one of real importance to the war was killed. The briefcase had been moved from its original place—where it would have killed Hitler—and rested behind a thick table leg, which protected him from the main force of the blast.

This attempt to assassinate Hitler was planned and carried out by several of his army generals and others who had once been close to him. Passionately patriotic, many of them secretly anti-Nazi long before, they believed he was leading their Germany to disaster.

Some of the men involved had been planning to kill Hitler for years; two earlier attempts had failed completely. They had drawn up plans for a new government after Hitler's death with anti-Nazi names in all important positions. They hoped for better terms of surrender from the Allies with that government in place.

The roundups of the men and women involved went on for months. An estimated four thousand people the Nazis believed to be conspirators were murdered. At Hitler's orders, the leaders who had not committed suicide were hanged in an especially cruel way and their death agonies filmed for his enjoyment. These men are greatly honored in Germany today. The key men in the plot were:

General Ludwig Beck
Carl Goerdeler
Ulrich von Hassell
General Friedrich Olbricht
Major General Hans Oster
General Claus Schenk Graf von Stauffenberg
Major General Hinning von Tresckow
General Erwin von Witzlebenn

The White Rose. In the summer of 1942 and early 1943, small mimeographed pamphlets appeared in the halls of the university of Munich. Others were dropped out of windows to people in the street, and still more were mailed to names picked at random. Headed LEAFLETS OF THE WHITE ROSE, they were written "to strive for the renewal of the mortally wounded German spirit." The people of Germany, they went on, had allowed themselves to be put into a "spiritual prison" by these "fascist criminals." Through apathy and tolerance of this "evil regime," each German was "guilty, guilty, guilty!" Later, the walls of the university were painted with FREEDOM! and DOWN WITH HITLER!

Hans Scholl and his sister Sophie, with their friend Christopher Probst and a few students, had written and distributed the leaflets. At first eager members of the Hitler Youth like all their friends, they had become disillusioned as they saw their liberties taken away—a loved book now forbidden reading, a favorite song now not to be sung. People they knew had "disappeared"; they had heard stories of concentration camps and mass murders from wounded soldiers on leave. They had decided it was necessary at last to resist the bloodying of the world and the destruction of Germany by hate and war.

Their "preparation for high treason," as the newspapers named it, had consisted of six leaflets that called for resistance in any form—from passive refusal to obey, to sabotage—against the Nazi regime. The three were caught, tried before a People's Court, denounced as criminals and traitors and sentenced to death. Sophie Scholl, twenty-one, Hans Scholl, twenty-four, and Christopher Probst, twenty-three, were beheaded on February 22, 1943. Hans's last words as he stood before his killer were "Long live freedom!"

Rosenstrasse. By February 1943 only 10,000 Jews remained alive in Berlin. Goebbels decided the time had come to make the city "cleansed of Jews." On the morning of February 27, police, Gestapo and SS arrested all of them. Taken to collection centers, 8,000 were deported to Auschwitz and murdered.

Nearly 2,000, however, were held in Rosenstrasse 2–4, a building that had been the Jewish community center in the heart of Berlin. These were Jews, almost entirely men, who were married to non-Jews. The Nazi plan was to exterminate them as they had the others. But they kept these men separate from the rest in order to temporarily calm the German citizens who were their wives. The Nazis thought that the women would believe the fate of these would be different from the 8,000 already deported.

Until that day, these couples had faced increasingly restrictive measures, their lives made almost unlivable in many ways. But by and large they had been allowed to remain together as a family unit. The wives were German citizens even if the Jewish men were not permitted to be, and the Nazis were afraid that forcing these mixed couples to separate would cause great social unrest.

First singly, then in small groups, the wives appeared in the street outside the building. They wanted information about their husbands, that was all. But none was given to them. Gradually the crowd grew. Joined by daughters and other female relatives, it sometimes numbered close to 6,000.

Each day for a week, these women appeared at Rosenstrasse and shouted in unison, "Give us back our husbands! Give us back our husbands!" A lineup of SS men with machine guns faced them instead. They threatened to shoot if the women did not leave. The women did not leave. They shouted, "Murderer! Murderer!" at the armed SS. They continued appearing each day, and each day they shouted together, "Give us back our husbands!"

The SS did not shoot. The women did not leave.

Goebbels noted in his diary on March 6, "There have been unpleasant scenes. . . . The people gathered together in large groups and even sided with the Jews to some extent."

On that same day, the 2,000 Jewish men were released.

Goebbels insisted that the protesters were civilians left homeless after British bombings of Berlin. He also said the Gestapo had made the arrests without his authority.

Leopold Gutterer, Goebbels's deputy, gave the true reason: "Goebbels released the Jews in order to eliminate the protest. . . . There was unrest, and it could have spread. . . . "

These Jewish men, whose German wives would not divorce or desert them, made up a large proportion of the Jews who survived the war in Germany.

The incident at Rosenstrasse was the only public German protest against the deportation of the Jews.

• • •

The White Rose Group. Hans Scholl, his sister Sophie and their friend Christopher Probst distributed six leaflets in Munich, Germany, calling for Germans to resist "the evil Nazi regime." They were beheaded for treason.

THE RIGHTEOUS AMONG THE NATIONS

Yad Vashem in Israel is the central worldwide organization devoted to the Holocaust. With its museum and huge archives, it is constantly involved in documentation and research on the period. Its central purpose is to serve as a perpetual memorial to the six million who perished.

A department within Yad Vashem seeks out the non-Jews who put their own lives in danger by saving Jews. Many mentioned in this chapter are among them. They are called the Righteous Among the Nations.

Placed against the death of six million, the number below is small. The courage, honesty and human decency involved is beyond measuring.

Poland	5,264	Switzerland	23
Netherlands	4,174	Moldova	31
France	1,786	Denmark	14
Ukraine	1,216	Bulgaria	13
Belgium	1,049	Great Britain	11
Hungary	475	Norway	7
Czech Republic + Slovakia	418	Sweden	7
Lithuania	414	Armenia	3
Russia + Belarus (Belorussia)	402	Spain	3
Germany	327	Estonia	2
Italy	240	Brazil	1
Greece	211	China	2
Yugoslavia (all countries)	189	Japan	1
Austria	82	Luxembourg	1
Latvia	65	Portugal	1
Romania	55	Turkey	1
Albania	53	USA	1
		Total Persons	15,670

The medal the Righteous receive from the government of Israel and Yad Vashem is inscribed with a quotation from the Talmud. It puts the importance of those who had the courage to care and the daring to act in a few simple words:

> "He who saves one life is considered as
> having saved the whole world."

15

IS THE HOLOCAUST UNIQUE?

> We are mad, not only individually but nationally. We must restrain manslaughter and isolated murders. But what of war, and the much-vaunted crime of slaughtering whole peoples?
>
> —Seneca, 8 B.C.(?)–A.D. 65

Is it possible to measure evil?

Is it less terrible to kill 150,000 people than it is to kill one million? Is it better in some way for "only" 30,000 people to die than two million? Six million? Is it easier to be killed by a bomb than a bullet? By a knife than by gas?

These are not foolish questions. They are among the kinds of things discussed when the topic is the Holocaust. Underlying the discussion is the fundamental question: Is the Holocaust unique? Has anything like it ever happened before—or since?

Trying to answer that requires a look back at history, but not very far back. Events over less than two hundred years ago offer examples of crimes against masses of people that, some believe, prove the Holocaust was only one among history's most terrible occurrences. The present day offers additional ones as well.

NATIVE AMERICANS—THE INDIANS

The United States underwent great expansion in the nineteenth century. The growing population spread and settled in areas that had been the homelands of Indian nations for many hundreds of years. The land was being taken from them piece by piece, often by force. The growth seemed unstoppable. In 1830 the Indian Removal Act was passed by Congress.

Thousands upon thousands of Indians in the Southeast and Southwest were forcibly rounded up and taken from their land by the federal government. They were to be resettled in areas set aside for them in Kansas, Nebraska and

Oklahoma. Guarded by the United States Army, they *walked*. Unaccustomed to the cold, hundreds froze to death. Others starved when their supplies ran out, still others died of disease. The Cherokees called their forced trek the "Trail of Tears." The Creek nation lost 40 percent of its population.

Among the Indian nations that were removed were the Seminole, Shawnee, Wyandot, Delaware, Cherokee, Chickasaw, Creek and Choctaw. This episode of American history marked the end of complex and rich cultures that had been in this land perhaps thousands of years before the arrival of the white man.

THE ARMENIANS

In the early years of the twentieth century, a movement for independence developed among the 2.5 million Christian Armenians in Muslim Turkey. Afraid they would aid the enemy during World War I, the Turkish government in 1915 ordered them expelled from their homes and deported to Palestine and Syria.

The army and police first rounded up all educated Armenians and slaughtered them, then went from village to village and did the same with all able-bodied males. The remaining leaderless old men, women and children were marched—on foot—across hundreds of miles of desert and mountains. They died of thirst, starvation and disease. Even more were massacred, as the able-bodied men had been, by soldiers and the police. It is estimated that close to 1.5 million Armenians died.

UKRAINE

Ukraine, when a Soviet republic, was the major source of grain for the USSR. During the 1930s, Soviet Premier Joseph Stalin ordered the changeover from individually owned farms to nationalized or collectively owned ones. The fiercely independent Ukrainians resisted and Stalin's secret police brought about the collectivization by force, killing thousands in the process. As punishment and to weaken any move toward independence, Stalin then ordered the bulk of Ukrainian wheat shipped out of the area and allowed none to be brought in.

Between 1932 and 1933 as many as nine million Ukrainians died of starvation. This, plus the continued crushing of nationalistic strivings that lasted until the 1940s, helps explain why so many Ukrainian villages welcomed the Nazis as liberators during World War II.

"THE RAPE OF NANKING"

Japan had been at war with China since 1931. On the morning of December 13, 1937, fifty thousand Japanese soldiers captured the city of Nanking, then the country's capital. Given the order to kill all captives, they proceeded to carry out a bloody massacre. The Chinese were used for target and bayonet practice. Japanese soldiers held decapitation contests. Men, women and children were forced to perform unspeakable acts before they were killed.

The massacre continued for approximately seven weeks. It is known to history as "The Rape of Nanking."

It is estimated that between 200,000 and 300,000 Chinese were killed during this period.

HIROSHIMA AND NAGASAKI

The first atomic bomb in history was dropped by American airmen on Hiroshima, Japan, on August 6, 1945. The single bomb leveled 90 percent of the city and killed an estimated 140,000 people. The second atomic bomb was dropped on the Japanese city of Nagasaki on August 9, 1945. More than one-third of the city was completely destroyed, and over 75,000 people were killed. These bombs were used, it is said, to bring World War II to a quicker end and to save thousands of American lives. The Japanese surrendered on August 14, 1945.

TIBET

As it had for centuries, Buddhism ruled the lives of the Tibetan people. Until the 1960s, approximately one-sixth of Tibetan men were priests or monks; both the religious and secular leaders were priests. Communist China invaded Tibet in 1950. In 1959 the people revolted, and the Chinese suppressed the rebellion by killing priests, monks and nuns, and destroying temples and religious shrines. They have continued their brutality to strengthen their control since then. Little information has been allowed to reach the West, so exact figures are unknown. But it is safe to say that thousands of temples have been destroyed. Out of a population of six million, the Chinese are believed to have slaughtered up to two million Tibetans.

CAMBODIA

Cambodia, a small country near Vietnam in Southeast Asia, was taken over by the Khmer Rouge communists in 1975. The leadership under Pol Pot was convinced that urban life was destructive to people and nation and wanted to rebuild the country based on the land—immediately.

All educated or westernized people were massacred. Buddhism, the major religion, was forbidden, temples destroyed and priests executed. The entire populations of all the cities were expelled from their homes, brutally moved and forced to live in the country as slave laborers. Conditions were unspeakable, the Khmer Rouge soldiers uncontrolled in their brutality. It is estimated that two million people died in the space of four years.

RWANDA

Rwanda is a Central African nation about the size of Maryland. Its two major population groups are the majority Hutu and the minority Tutsi people. Over most of the area's history, the Tutsis held power.

In 1962 the Hutus gained control. In 1973 Juvenal Habayarimana took over the presidency.

Habayarimana's family and Hutus from his home area were given high-ranking positions. Now Hutus received preference in government, the military and in public service. Tutsis were excluded from positions of power, from educational opportunities, often from the ability to earn a decent living.

For these and other reasons, many of which lay farther back in their history, the tension between the two groups was intense. Unrest was growing; so was a movement toward greater democracy. Radical Hutus resisted both.

On April 6, 1994, a plane carrying President Habayarimana was shot down and he was killed. The radical Hutus had already made plans for organized Tutsi murder at the hands of the Hutu populace. At the death of Habayarimana, the killings began.

From that date and for one hundred days thereafter, Tutsis were butchered throughout the country.

By mid-May, the International Red Cross estimated 500,000 people had been killed. It was destruction of a single group on a scale not seen since World War II. This was genocide.

The world knew and condemned it. But no government or official body, including the United States and the United Nations, called the massacres genocide. If the murders had been officially identified as genocide of the Tutsis, the UN and its member nations would have been required by international law—written after the Holocaust—to "prevent and punish" the perpetrators. They called the murders such things as "calamitous events" and acts of "tribal hatreds" rather than genocide. And they argued about "solving other people's problems" and "expenses." They would not call it genocide.

The slaughter came to its end mid-July 1994.

In a little over three months, nearly one million Rwandans had been murdered. Over one-third of the Tutsis in the world had been killed.

Yugoslavia: "Ethnic Cleansing" in the Balkans

After World War II, Yugoslavia was united into a nation of six republics—Serbia, Slovenia, Croatia, Bosnia and Hercegovina, Montenegro, and Macedonia—all under the leadership of Serbia.

Slobodan Milosevic became president of Serbia in 1989. With a vision of a "greater Serbia," he believed areas adjoining Serbia should be made all-Serb. Any drive toward independence within the other republics was intolerable.

Slovenia, economically the strongest of the other republics, broke away in 1991. Milosevic sent in troops, but the war there was over in a few days.

Croatia was next to break away. Its battles with Serbia in 1991 and 1992 were followed by a 1995 Croatian campaign of "ethnic cleansing" that ousted Serbs from Croatia and western Bosnia.

In 1992 Bosnia declared independence. The Serbian army invaded. At

Milosevic's bidding, the army also began a campaign to get rid of all Muslims in Bosnia. Only Orthodox Christian Serbs were to remain. International pressure forced Milosevic to order his army out. But the majority of the army was made up of Bosnian Serbs who stayed behind and were joined by other Serbs still living in Bosnia. They proceeded to carry out a campaign of "ethnic cleansing" to eliminate Muslims from Bosnia completely. The result was the bloodiest Balkan episode since Nazi occupation in World War II.

Peace was brought about with the help of the United Nations. But that was not the end. Kosovo, a province of Serbia, was the next area of "ethnic cleansing." Again, at Milosevic's bidding; again, a peace accord of sorts was drawn up with the help of the United Nations.

The Serbian people voted Milosevic out of office in 2000. Declared a war criminal, he now stands trial before the International Criminal Tribunal for the Former Yugoslavia, a court established by the UN in 1993. No verdict has yet been reached.

Macedonia became independent without a fight in 1992. But violence began there in 2001, when ethnic Albanians living in the country demanded greater power. Peace efforts inch forward, but at this writing the fighting has increased and shows little sign of slowing.

Montenegro has remained part of Serbia, but at this time a strong movement toward independence is growing steadily.

The total number killed in these wars of the late twentieth and early twenty-first centuries is unknown. In Bosnia alone, 250,000 or more are dead. Refugees forced or fleeing from their homes number at least three million.

All of the major groups that make up the Balkans have been involved in hatred, bloodshed and war for centuries. The reasons are too complex to describe here. But it is safe to say that, at one time or another, each sizable group in the area has tried to "cleanse" one area or another of "undesirable" other groups.

That has worked out to be one another.

THE UNIQUENESS OF THE HOLOCAUST

That is enough. It is not necessary to mention the endless border war between the two starving countries of Ethiopia and Eritrea, nor the massacre of Tamils by Hindus and of Hindus by Tamils in Sri Lanka. No, not the Protestant-Catholic killings in Northern Ireland, nor the mounting murders of Palestinians and Israelis. Not even the deaths of thousands in suicide attacks on New York City and Washington, D.C.

History is full of horrors. This is not a contest to win some awful prize for evil.

How, then, in light of all this, is the murder of six million European Jews different? What is it about that event that makes it stand alone in history?

Among many historians of the period, two seem to have answered that question once and for all. The first historian, Eberhard Jäckel, is German.

"Never before had any state, with all the authority of its responsible leader, decided and announced that it intended to kill off a particular group of human beings, including the old, the women, the children and the sucklings, as completely as possible, and had then translated this decision into action with every possible . . . power at the state's command."

The second historian, Lucy S. Dawidowicz, is American.

Echoing Jäckel, she said: "Never before in human history had a state and a political movement dedicated itself to the destruction of a whole people."

She goes on:

"In every case of terrible human destructiveness that we have known, . . . killing was not an end in itself, but a means to an end. . . .

"[But] the German dictatorship murdered the Jews for the sake of murdering the Jews. For the Germans [took] to themselves the decision as to who was entitled to live on this earth and who was not.

"That is the uniqueness of the Holocaust."

16

THE FINISH

We were free, but we did not know it, did not believe it, could not believe it. We had waited for this such long days and nights that now when the dream had come true it still seemed a dream.
—Mosche Sandberg, Birkenau survivor

THE NUMBER OF JEWISH DEAD

THE EXACT NUMBER OF JEWS KILLED IN THE HOLOCAUST will never be known. Nazi records are incomplete, have been destroyed or cannot be found. They did not keep precise track of the masses who were marched straight from the deportation trains to the gas chambers. Babies were not always recorded individually either. Newborn infants were killed before their births could be registered, and their numbers cannot even be guessed.

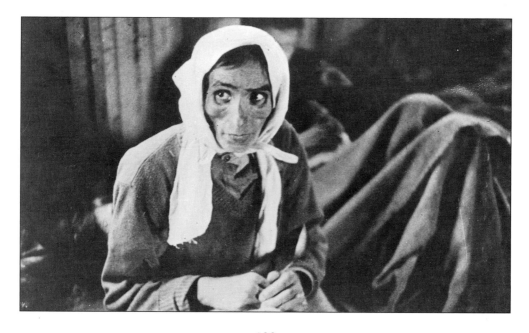

The most common method used to arrive at the figures is to take the numbers of survivors from each country, and then to subtract that from the population before the war. But sometimes the exact number of survivors is hard to find and the population figures are very old or not accurate.

For these and other reasons, the true number of Jewish dead remains unknown. All figures are only estimates. Many historians believe that the number may be higher than six million.

The table that follows is largely based on figures compiled by Yad Vashem.

Poland	3,000,000
Soviet Union	1,316,000
Hungary	569,000
Romania	287,000
Czechoslovakia	149,150
Germany	141,000
Netherlands	100,000
France	77,320
Greece	67,000
Yugoslavia	63,300
Austria	50,000
Belgium	28,900
Italy	7,500
Luxembourg	1,950
Norway	762
Denmark	51
Finland	7
Total	5,858,940

THE SURVIVORS

Germany surrendered on May 7, 1945. The war in Europe was over. The prisoners were freed.

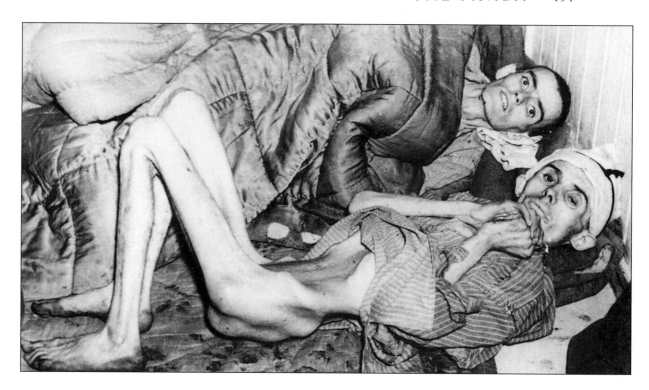

The gates were opened. Europe swarmed with millions of people set free from labor camps, jails and concentration camps, joined by the multitude of workers deported to Germany for forced labor. Thousands of miles from their home countries, they were housed in camps set up for them, the displaced persons', or DP, camps.

An enormous operation was begun by the Western Allies, the United Nations Relief and Rehabilitation Agency and other agencies to get these people home. In little more than a year, most had returned to their countries to begin new lives in a new and better time.

The Nazis had reserved "special handling" for the Jews before and during the war. Now, with freedom, their situation remained different as well.

As the Allies liberated the camps, they found tens of thousands of unburied bodies of the dead. Those left alive were remnants of human beings, so sick, so starved and weak, they could not even survive being free. "Many died from sheer joy," reported a witness. "They had lived on hope, on fear and on their sheer nerves for so long that the sudden relaxation, when it came, was too much for them."

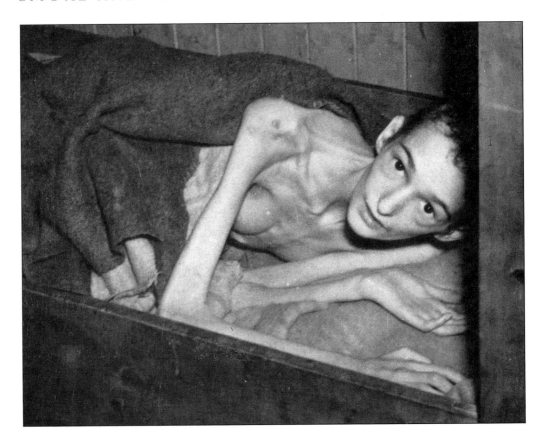

They were fed. But they had been starved for so long that some of them could not eat anymore. Hundreds died from the first food given to them. Their feeble beaten bodies could not deal with such "richness" as powdered milk, some sugar, some salt, oatmeal and canned meat. Doctors reported that the average prisoner weighed between sixty and eighty pounds. They had lost 50 to 60 percent of their body weight and inches off their normal height.

In the areas freed by the Americans, French and British, 60,000 Jews were found alive. Within one week, 20,000 had died. At the Bergen-Belsen camp in Germany, the count was 500 each day.

An American reporter had visited the gas chambers and the crematoriums and had seen the torture rooms and shooting chambers. He had spoken to these tortured skeletons of the living and had seen the tangled bodies of the dead. He wrote, "We had known. The world had vaguely heard. But until now no one of us had looked on this. . . . It was as though we had penetrated at last to the center of the black heart, to the very crawling inside of the vicious heart."

Survivors in Western Europe were soon joined by those from Eastern Europe. The number of homeless Jews grew to over 300,000. Many of them had to learn that they were the only ones left alive from a large family, sometimes the last from an entire community, whose neighboring community was completely destroyed. Their past lives had vanished in the whirlwind of the Holocaust. Now they had no home.

Survivors from Germany and Austria did not want to return. Neither did those from Eastern Europe, the center of the worst of the Nazi horror. New horror was there as well. Over five hundred Jews who returned to Poland were killed by Poles between May and December 1945, after the war was over and the Nazis had gone.

Most of the countries occupied by the Nazis were not strong enough to accept thousands of new immigrants, particularly since nearly all were sick in body and in mind and needed care. The United States did not relax its immigration laws. Neither did Great Britain. England also refused to allow

These children were found in Birkenau, alive and in comparatively good health. It is believed they were being held for medical experiments.

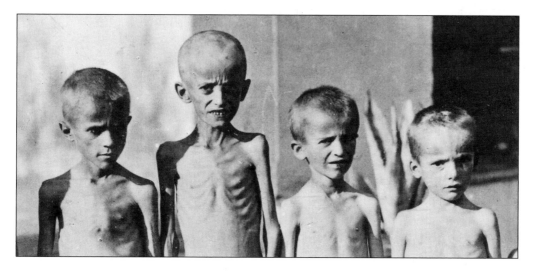

more than its small 1939 monthly quota of Jews into Palestine. It was a familiar situation: there was no place to put these Jews.

By this time the survivors in the DP camps were being treated well. President Harry S. Truman insisted, and General of the Army Dwight D.

Eisenhower made sure, that as much as humanly possible was done for them. Such organizations as the United Nations, the Quakers, the International Red Cross and several Jewish relief agencies spared nothing in their efforts to restore them to a decent life. They helped survivors begin anew in other countries, when the other countries would have them.

Overwhelmingly, the survivors wanted to go to Palestine. Since it could not be done legally, it was done illegally. A Jewish group based in Palestine, the Mossad arm of the secret defense army Haganah, managed to "find"

Liberation by the U.S. Army came too late.

Harry S. Truman, President of the United States 1945–1953. His pressure on the British and the American vote in the United Nations marked the turning point in the creation of the State of Israel.

sixty-five ships. Between 1945 and 1948, almost 200,000 survivors of the Holocaust were brought to Palestine. The true healing had begun.

HOPE

This is not the place to give a history of events after World War II. Let it be enough to say that it took time, much pain and great determination from Jews and non-Jews alike. Pressure from the president of the United States marked the turning point. Three years after the end of the Holocaust, a Jewish homeland came into being. For the first time in over two thousand years the Jews had something that was theirs, and theirs as Jews.

On May 14, 1948, the State of Israel was born.

No longer worn as a yellow badge of shame, the Star of David flew as the flag of the Jewish nation.

17

JUSTICE

I have never personally hated the Jews . . . But Himmler had ordered it and had even explained the necessity, and I never really gave much thought to whether it was wrong.

—Rudolf Hoess, Commander of Auschwitz, where over 1.5 million Jews were killed

Question: Did you prefer to be a party to wholesale murder rather than be arrested yourself?
Answer: Yes.

—From the trial of Josef Kramer, Commander of Bergen-Belsen concentration camp, known as the "Beast of Belsen"

In 1943 the United Nations established the War Crimes Commission. Its purpose was to investigate the crimes committed by Nazi Germany and to name the individuals responsible for them. The commission also identified several organizations as criminal—the SS, SA, Gestapo and the leadership of the Nazi party, and the like. Participation in any of these groups was itself a crime.

Eventually three major categories of crimes were defined:

Crimes against peace. Planning, preparing, starting or waging a war of aggression, or participating in a plan for such a war.
War crimes. The murder, ill-treatment or deportation to slave labor of civilians in occupied territory, the murder or ill-treatment of prisoners of war, the killing of hostages, the destruction of cities, towns and so on, not justified by military need.
Crimes against humanity. The murder, extermination, enslavement, deportation and other inhuman acts committed against civilian groups on the basis of religion, race or politics.

The Holocaust and the Final Solution fall mainly into the third category of crimes and somewhat less into the second.

The UN commission eventually developed the International Military Tribunal. Representatives of the four major Allied powers—the United States, Great Britain, France and the USSR—named the accused and defined their crimes.

The tribunal met in the Palace of Justice in Nuremberg, Germany, on November 20, 1945. Four prosecutors from each of the Allied nations presented the case against the accused. Twenty-two leading members of the Third Reich were put on trial.

The accused in the courtroom at Nuremberg. In the first row of the dock, Goering is seated far left, beside Rudolf Hess, Hitler's former right-hand man. Third from the right is Julius Streicher, owner and publisher of Der Stürmer. *Fifth from the right is Hans Frank, governor of Nazi-occupied Poland.*

The accused were allowed to choose lawyers, who defended them, brought evidence on their behalf and cross-examined witnesses. The trials were conducted according to law; they were as fair as possible. That was more than these men ever allowed the millions killed at their instructions.

The trials came to an end on October 1, 1946, incidentally the most solemn religious holiday in the Jewish calendar—Yom Kippur, the Day of Atonement. Twelve of the twenty-two accused had been sentenced to death, three to life imprisonment, four to prison terms of shorter length, and three were found innocent of the charges against them and freed.

All but two had pleaded "Not guilty." Their defense: They were only following orders.

The original International Military Tribunal did not continue after the first trials because of disagreements among the four Allied nations. But other trials were held in all the occupied countries, and eventually in Germany under German law as well. Between the war's end in 1945 and 1949, in the section of the country that came to be called West Germany, almost 10,000 people were tried by Allied and German courts for Nazi crimes. There are occasional trials today in almost all of Europe, when a participant in the Holocaust is identified or discovered.

Nazis who were punished lightly or escaped punishment entirely are old now, and many have died of natural causes. Others who fled after the war lived in peace in various countries until their eventual capture or death, and some continue to do so. Josef Mengele lived in Paraguay until his death in a swimming accident in 1977, for example; Erich Priebke stayed in Argentina until brought to trial in Rome in 1998; at this writing Alois Brunner is believed to be living undisturbed in Syria.

Many lesser Nazis live in other countries, including the United States. Some have been caught—Nacelles Scoffer, for example, a sadistic guard at many camps, lied about his past, became an American citizen in 1958, and lived as a baker in Pennsylvania until his deportation to Romania in January 2000. There are many others, known and unknown, throughout the world.

The question of whether justice has been done is continually argued about to this day.

The remainder of this chapter is made up of a listing of some of the men and women directly involved in the Holocaust and in the carrying out of the

Final Solution. The information includes the actions connected with the Holocaust, whether the accused was brought to trial, the date of the trial, the verdict and how the verdict was carried out.

Has justice been done? The information given here may help in finding the answer.

Auerswald, Heinz. Commissioner of Warsaw ghetto. Responsible for its daily operation. Not placed on trial. Died of natural causes, date unknown.

Bach-Zelewski, Erich. Higher SS and police leader in Central Russia and chief of antipartisan units. After 35,000 people had been executed, he wrote, "There is not a Jew left in Estonia." Responsible for many other atrocities. In 1962 sentenced to life imprisonment for Hitler-ordered murder of German civilians. No mention of wartime role during trial. Died in prison.

Baer, Richard. Commander of Auschwitz I. Died before trial, 1963.

Barbie, Klaus. Gestapo chief in Lyons, France. Known as "The Butcher of Lyons." Responsible for the torture, murder and deportation of Jewish children and adults. Worked for the U.S. Army, 1947 to 1951. Lived in Peru and Bolivia, 1951 to 1983. Brought to trial in France and sentenced to life imprisonment, 1987. Died in prison, 1991.

Irma Grese, former guard at Belsen. Her sadistic cruelty toward the prisoners and the ease with which she sent thousands to the gas chambers earned her the nickname "Bitch of Belsen."

Berger, Gottlob. SS Main Office. One of Himmler's foremost experts on racial selection and his liaison with offices for the Occupied Eastern Territories. Sentenced to twenty-five years. Sentence reduced to ten years. Freed, 1951.

Best, Werner. Commissioner for occupied Denmark, senior SS and Nazi police leader. Condemned to death by Danish court. Sentence commuted to five years. Found guilty of mass murder by German court, 1958. Freed, 1971.

Biberstein, Ernst. Special Action Group C. Condemned to death. Sentence reduced to life imprisonment.

Biebow, Hans. Lodz ghetto administration. Executed, 1947.

Blobel, Paul. Special Action Group C. Responsible for the murder of over 60,000 Jews in Ukraine, 35,000 at Babi Yar alone; directed Commando 1005, Operation Blotout, whose purpose was to dig up bodies of Jews and others and burn them to remove evidence of slaughter. Executed, 1951.

Blume, Walter. Special Action Group C. Executed, 1947.

Bormann, Martin. Head of the main Nazi party office and Hitler's private secretary. In the last few years of the war he acquired great power and often spoke in the Führer's name. Killed in the Battle of Berlin, 1945.

Bothmann, Hans. Commander of Chelmno death camp. Suicide, 1946.

Böttcher, Herbert. SS and police leader, Radom, Poland. Executed, 1952.

Brack, Victor. SS colonel and a top official in the Reich Main Office. Active in the construction of Polish death camps. In charge of Operation T4, the "mercy killing" of at least 100,000 Germans judged unfit for life. Set up mobile gassing vans in Riga and Minsk to exterminate Jews judged "unsuitable for work." Executed, 1948.

Brandt, Karl. Hitler's personal physician and one of the main doctors involved in Operation T4, the euthanasia program. Executed, 1948.

Braune, Werner. Special Action Group D. Executed, 1951.

Brunner, Alois. SS deportation expert in Vienna, Berlin, Salonika, France and Slovakia. Reported living in Syria, 2000.

Brunner, Anton. Gestapo, Vienna. Executed, 1946.

Bühler, Josef. General Government. Executed, 1948.

Daluege, Kurt. Commander in chief of the Order Police and later deputy protector of Bohemia and Moravia. Responsible for the destruction of the

Adolf Eichmann, the man whose efficient organization made the deportations possible. He is reported to have said: "I laugh when I jump into the grave, because of the feeling that I have killed five million Jews. That gives me great satisfaction and gratification."

town of Lidice in revenge for Heydrich's assassination and other terrorist measures against the Czechs. Executed, 1946.

Dannecker, Theodor. SS captain in charge of the deportation of Jews to Auschwitz from France, Bulgaria and Italy. Suicide, 1945.

Ehrlinger, Erich. Special Action Group A. Sentenced to twelve years.

Eichmann, Adolf. SS lieutenant colonel, chief of SS Department of Jewish Affairs, Bureau IVB-4. Responsible for arranging and coordinating all transportation of Jews to the camps throughout the period of the Final Solution. Captured by Israeli agents in Argentina, where he had lived since 1946. Tried in Israel, 1960. Executed, 1962.

Eicke, Theodor. SS general and inspector of concentration camps and SS concentration camp guard formations. Used Dachau and its prisoners as a training school for concentration camp guards, laying down exact instructions on punishment, beatings, solitary confinement and shooting of prisoners. Killed in action, 1943.

Fendler, Lothar. Special Action Group C. Sentenced to ten years. Sentence reduced to eight years.

Flick, Friedrich. Wealthy industrialist, supporter of the Nazi movement and one of the most prominent employers of slave labor in the Third Reich. Bought and used 48,000 slave laborers, 80 percent of whom died. Jewish concentration camp inmates were often sent to work in his various munitions plants. Died in Konstanz, West Germany, on July 20, 1972, at the age of ninety, leaving a fortune of more than $1.5 billion.

Frank, Hans. Governor of Poland during World War II. Sentenced to death and hanged, 1946.

Frick, Wilhelm. Reich minister of the interior from 1933 to 1943. Responsible for setting up the laws that eliminated Jews from German life, climaxing in the Nuremberg Laws. Executed, 1946.

Fuchs, Wilhelm. Special Action Group in Serbia. Executed, 1946.

Fünten, Ferdinand aus der. Central Office for Jewish Emigration in Holland. Condemned to death. Sentence reduced to life imprisonment.

Gemmecker, Albert Konrad. Commander of Westerbork, Holland, transit camp for deported Dutch Jews. Believed to be living in Germany.

Globke, Hans. Reich Ministry of the Interior. Coauthored an official explanation of the Nuremberg Laws, making it clear that all Jews were automatically denied citizenship. Invented the idea of compelling all German Jews to adopt the middle names of "Israel" and "Sarah." After the war he was appointed state secretary of the West German government and chief of its personnel division. Died of natural causes, 1973.

Globocnik, Odilo. SS lieutenant general in charge of Operation Reinhard, the plan for the extermination of Polish Jews. Suicide, 1945.

Gluecks, Richard. SS general and inspector of concentration camps. Believed a suicide, 1945.

Goebbels, Joseph. Minister of propaganda. Responsible for keeping the press, theater, radio and all published works in line with Nazi ideas. Main organizer of Kristallnacht pogrom of 1938 in Germany. One of the chief supporters of the Final Solution, personally supervising the deportation of Jews from Berlin. Committed suicide with Hitler at war's end, 1945.

Goering, Hermann. Commander in chief of the German air force, president of the Reichstag, prime minister of Prussia and, as Hitler's chosen successor, officially second in command in the Third Reich. Creator of the Gestapo. It was his idea to fine the German Jewish community a billion marks after the 1938 Kristallnacht pogrom. Ordered the elimination of Jews from the German economy, the "Aryanization" of their property and businesses, and their exclusion from schools, resorts, parks, forests and so on. Wrote the order to Heydrich to carry out all preparations for "The Final Solution of the Jewish Question." Sentenced to death by hanging. Suicide, 1946.

Hensch, Walter. Special Action Group C. Condemned to death. Sentence reduced to fifteen years.

Hess, Rudolf. Deputy leader of the Nazi party and number three man in Nazi Germany. Helped Hitler write *Mein Kampf.* On May 10, 1941, Hess secretly left Germany on a solo flight to Great Britain hoping to convince the British government that Hitler wanted peace with England, a free hand in Eastern Europe and a combined fight against Russia. Sentenced to life imprisonment. Suicide in prison, 1987.

Heyde, Werner. Head of the Reich Association for Hospitals and Sanatoria. Ensured their cooperation in Operation T4, the "mercy killing" of 100,000 Germans judged "unworthy of life." Sentenced to death in 1946; escaped. Gave himself up in 1959. Suicide, 1964.

Heydrich, Reinhard. Head of the Reich Security Main Office and the leading architect of the Final Solution. Known as the "Blond Beast" and "The Man with the Iron Heart." Assassinated May 27, 1942, in Czechoslovakia. The Germans razed to the ground the entire village of Lidice in revenge, executing all of its male inhabitants and deporting the women and children to concentration camps.

Hildebrandt, Richard. Higher SS and police leader, Danzig. Sentenced to twenty-five years. Freed, 1955.

Himmler, Heinrich. Chief of the SS, head of the Gestapo, minister of the interior from 1943 to 1945 and the second most powerful man in wartime Germany. Supreme overseer of the Final Solution. Suicide, 1945.

Hitler, Adolf. The supreme leader of Nazi Germany. Rescued German pride lost after World War I and turned the country into an absolute dictatorship under the control of the Nazi party, over which he had complete control. Started World War II, built the most powerful armed forces the world had ever known and conquered most of Europe. Believed Jews were responsible for all evil in the world and decreed their extermination. The Final Solution was put into effect at his order and resulted in the killing of six million European Jews. Committed suicide at war's end in 1945, in his last will and testament calling "international Jewry" the "universal poisoner of all peoples."

Hoess, Rudolf. Commander of Auschwitz, 1940 to 1943. Noted in his memoirs that "Auschwitz became the greatest human extermination center of all time"—over one million Jews were killed there. Executed, 1947.

Höfle, Hermann. Office of the SS and police leader, Lublin, Poland. Arrested, 1961. Suicide, 1962.

Höfle, Hermann. Higher SS and police leader, Slovakia. Executed, 1948.

Hössler, Franz. Auschwitz administrator. Executed, 1945.

Hoven, Waldemar. Camp doctor, Buchenwald. Executed, 1948.

Jäger, Karl. Special Action Group 3, Lithuania. Suicide, 1959.

Jeckeln, Friedrich. Higher SS and police leader, Ostland, the Nazi name for a German "colony" made up of occupied Estonia, Latvia, Lithuania and Belorussia. Executed, 1946.

Jost, Heinz. Commander of Special Action Group A. Sentenced to life imprisonment; sentence reduced to ten years. Fined 15,000 reichsmarks, approximately two thousand dollars at the time.

Kaltenbrunner, Ernst. Chief of the Reich Security Main Office after Heydrich's assassination. Controlled the Gestapo, the concentration camp system and the administration of the Final Solution. Executed, 1946.

Katzmann, Fritz. SS and police leader in Galicia, Poland. Died of natural causes, 1957.

Keitel, Wilhelm. General field marshal and chief of staff of the High Command of the Armed Forces. Second to Hitler in command of the armed forces. Justified the massacres by Special Action Groups in Russia and said, "Any act of mercy is a crime against the German people." Executed, 1946.

Klein, Fritz. Auschwitz camp doctor. Executed, 1945.

Koch, Erich. Reich commissioner of Ukraine, 1941 to 1944. Caused the deaths of hundreds of thousands of Jews and non-Jews, their deportation to concentration camps and the razing of their villages. Condemned to death, 1959. Execution postponed indefinitely because of continuing illness. Died in prison, 1986.

Koch, Ilse. SS officer and guard at Buchenwald concentration camp and wife of the commander, Karl Koch. Known as the "Bitch of Buchenwald" for her sadistic cruelty toward prisoners. Sentenced to life imprisonment, 1947; sentence reduced to four years; released. Arrested again in 1949 for the killing of German citizens in the camp. Sentenced to life imprisonment, 1951. Suicide, 1967.

Koppe, Wilhelm. Higher SS and police leader in Wartheland, a Nazi-named section of Poland, and also in the General Government. Was to be brought to trial in 1964. Trial not held because of ill health.

Kramer, Josef. Commander of Birkenau and Bergen-Belsen camps. Known as the "Beast of Belsen" for his sadistic cruelty toward prisoners. Executed, 1945.

Krüger, Friedrich. Higher SS and police leader, General Government. Reported killed in action, 1945.

Krumey, Hermann. Special Action Group "Eichmann." Sentenced to five years, 1965.

Krupp, Alfred. In sole control of Krupp industries, the largest producer of guns, tanks and ammunition in the Third Reich. Used over 100,000 slave laborers, including Jews from Auschwitz and elsewhere, of which 70,000 to 80,000 died. Krupp family members were early supporters of Hitler and gave 10 million reichsmarks a year to the Nazis. Sentenced to twelve years and the loss of all money and property, 1948. Freed, 1951. All property and personal fortune, estimated at over $150 million, returned to him. Died of natural causes, 1967.

Krupp, Gustav. Father of Alfred, with whom he worked. *See* Alfred Krupp entry for details. Not tried because of ill health. Died of natural causes, 1950.

Liebehenschel, Arthur. Commander of Auschwitz. Executed, 1948.

Lohse, Heinrich. Reich commissioner for the Baltic States and White Russia during the most brutal period of the Final Solution. Sentenced to ten years, 1948. Freed, 1951. Died of natural causes, 1964.

Mengele, Josef. Chief medical officer at Birkenau, Auschwitz killing center. In charge of selection of Jews for the gas chambers, conducted horrifying medical experiments, particularly on twins. Escaped to Argentina at war's end. Also lived in Brazil and Paraguay. Died in a swimming accident in Paraguay, 1977. Body identified as Mengele in 1985.

Müller, Heinrich. Head of the Gestapo. As Adolf Eichmann's direct superior, signed order for the immediate delivery to Auschwitz of 45,000 Jews for extermination, and countless other orders of the same kind. Last seen April 1945. Fate unknown.

Naumann, Erich. Commander of Special Action Group B. Executed, 1951.

Nebe, Arthur. SS general, chief of criminal police, commander of Special Action Group B; part of July 20th Plot against Hitler. According to official records, executed in 1945, but believed seen in Ireland, 1960.

Nosske, Gustav. Special Action Group D. Sentenced to life imprisonment; sentence reduced to ten years.

Novak, Franz. Assistant to Adolf Eichmann. Organized transport of tens of thousands of Jews to the camps. Sentenced to eight years, 1964. New trial, acquitted, 1966. Retried, sentenced to nine years, 1969. Retried again, sentenced to seven years, 1972.

Oberg, Karl. SS and police leader, Radom, Poland, and supreme head of the SS and police in occupied France, where he took part in the extermination of Jews. Responsible for the Jewish Yellow Star decree in occupied France. Sentenced to death, 1954. Freed, 1962. Died of natural causes, 1965.

Ohlendorf, Otto. Commander of Special Action Group D, later chief of security service of the Reich Security Main Office. Organizer of mass murders in southern Ukraine 1941 to 1942. Executed, 1951.

Ott, Adolf. Special Action Group B. Condemned to death. Sentence reduced to life imprisonment.

Pohl, Oswald. Chief of the SS Economic and Administrative Department in charge of the "economic" side of the Final Solution, in which all valuables seized from gassed Jews—including clothing, human hair, gold tooth fillings and gold spectacles—were sent back to Germany. Executed, 1951.

Priebke, Erich. SS captain. Ordered to collect as reprisal ten Italians for each of the 33 Germans killed by partisans, he brought 335—two more than ordered—to a cave outside of Rome, many Jews among them. Each was shot in the back of the neck. The Ardeatine Caves massacre is the worst mass murder of civilians in wartime Italy. Found living under his own name in a small town in Argentina, Priebke was brought to trial in Rome and sentenced to life imprisonment, 1998.

Rademacher, Franz. "Jewish expert" in the German Foreign Office. Drew up the plan to deport all Jews to the French island of Madagascar, which was canceled with the takeover of Poland and invasion of Russia. His name appears on countless orders concerning the deportation of Jews to the death camps. Supervised the murder of Jews in Yugoslavia in 1941. Sentenced to three years and five months, 1952. Fled to Syria before imprisonment. Returned voluntarily to Germany, 1966. Sentenced to five years in 1968 but then released because of "poor health." Died of natural causes, 1973.

Radetzky, Waldermar von. Special Action Group B. Sentenced to twenty years. Sentence reduced to time served, 1951.

Rahm, Karl. Commander of Theresienstadt concentration camp. Executed, 1947.

Rapp, Albert. Special Action Group B. Sentenced to life imprisonment, 1965.

Rasch, Otto. Commander of Special Action Group C. Indicted; too ill to be tried.

Rascher, Sigmund. Medical experimenter in Dachau concentration camp. Rumored shot in Dachau, 1945.

Rauter, Hans Albin. Higher SS and police leader, Holland. Executed, 1949.

Richter, Gustav. SS deportation expert in Romania. Reported living in Stuttgart, Germany.

Rosenberg, Alfred. Minister for the Occupied Eastern Territories. Executed, 1946.

Ruehl, Felix. Special Action Group D. Sentenced to ten years. Sentence reduced to time served.

Sammern-Frankenegg, Ferdinand von. SS and police leader, Warsaw. Killed by partisans in Yugoslavia, 1944.

Sandberger, Martin. Special Action Group A. Condemned to death. Sentence reduced to life imprisonment.

Sauckel, Fritz. In charge of labor mobilization for the Third Reich. Responsible for the deaths of tens of thousands of Jewish workers in Poland and for deporting five million people from their homes in occupied territories to work as slave labor in Germany. Executed, 1946.

Schirach, Baldur von. Reich youth leader and governor of Vienna. Sentenced to twenty years. Freed, 1966. Died of natural causes, 1974.

Schubert, Heinz Hermann. Special Action Group D. Condemned to death. Sentence reduced to ten years.

Schulz, Erwin. Special Action Group C. Sentenced to twenty years. Sentence reduced to fifteen years. Freed, 1954.

Seibert, Willi. Special Action Group D. Condemned to death. Sentence reduced to fifteen years.

Seyss-Inquart, Artur von. Reich governor of Austria, deputy to Hans Frank, the governor of Nazi-occupied Poland, and Reich commissioner of German-occupied Netherlands. Executed, 1946.

Speer, Albert. Reich minister for armaments and war production. Admitted responsibility for slave labor in the factories under his control and for using SS-supplied concentration camp prisoners for his production lines. Sentenced to twenty years imprisonment, 1946. Freed, 1966. Died of natural causes, 1981.

Sporrenberg, Jakob. SS and police leader, Lublin, Poland. Executed, 1950.

Stahlecker, Franz Walter. Commander of Special Action Group A. Killed in action, 1942.

Stangl, Franz. Commander of Sobibor death camp, then commander of Treblinka death camp from 1942 to 1943. Fled to Syria, 1948, then to Brazil, 1951 to 1967. Brought to Germany from there and sentenced to life imprisonment, 1970. Died of natural causes, 1971.

Steimle, Eugen. Special Action Group B. Condemned to death. Sentence reduced to twenty years. Freed, 1954.

Strauch, Eduard. Special Action Group A. Condemned to death. Execution stayed because of defendant's insanity.

Streicher, Julius. Fanatic anti-Semite and a favorite of Hitler. Owner and publisher of the extremely popular newspaper *Der Stürmer* (The Great Storm), which used as its banner THE JEWS ARE OUR MISFORTUNE and printed stories of Jewish ritual murders, sex crimes and other lies. An early follower of Hitler, Streicher constantly called for extermination of the Jews both in his newspaper and in his frequent speeches, which attracted very large audiences. Called his death sentence "a triumph for world Jewry." Executed, 1946.

Stroop, Jürgen. SS and police leader, Warsaw. Responsible for the defeat of the Warsaw ghetto uprising in 1943 and the destruction of the ghetto. Executed, 1951.

Terboven, Josef. Reich commissioner in Norway. Suicide, 1945.

Thierack, Otto. Reich minister of justice, SS major general. Drafted the "extermination through work" decrees, put into effect against Jewish concentration camp prisoners. Suicide, 1946.

Vallat, Xavier. Anti-Jewish commissioner, France. Sentenced to ten years. Freed, 1950.

Veesenmayer, Edmund. Reich minister to Hungary. Worked with Eichmann and Kaltenbrunner on Final Solution in Hungary and Slovakia. Sentenced to twenty years. Sentence reduced to ten years. Freed, 1951.

Wächter, Otto. Governor of Galicia, Poland. Died in Rome, Italy, of natural causes, 1949. Never brought to trial.

Wendler, Richard. Governor of Cracow District. Not tried. Lived and worked as an attorney in Germany after the war.

Winkelmann, Otto. Higher SS and police leader in Hungary. Not tried. Became a city councilor in Kiel, Germany, after the war.

Wirth, Christian. Administrative head of Operation T4, the "mercy killing" program in Germany. Assigned to begin extermination of Jews in Chelmno death camp. In charge of the extermination squads at Belzec, Sobibor and Treblinka death camps. Killed by partisans, 1944.

Wisliceny, Dieter. SS deportation expert in Slovakia, Greece and Hungary. Executed, 1948.

Wolff, Karl. Chief SS and police commander in Italy and chief of Heinrich Himmler's personal staff. Sentenced to four years hard labor in 1946; spent one week in prison. Arrested again in 1962, accused of sending at least 300,000 Jews to Treblinka and of other involvement in the Final Solution. Sentenced to fifteen years. Freed, 1971. Died of natural causes, 1984.

18

THE TIME IS NOW

The world is too dangerous to live in—not because of the people who do evil, but because of the people who sit and let it happen.

—Albert Einstein

It is tempting to think that nothing like the Holocaust can happen again. Nazi Germany lost the war. Most major Nazis are dead, or have been found guilty in a court of law. Israel, the Jewish state, has a population of over five million. Other Jews live mostly in peace around the world. The United States alone has a population of more than six million Jews.

So the worst is over, everything has been taken care of, and there is nothing to worry about anymore. Time to sit back and relax.

Not so. Not yet.

HATE GROUPS

The hatred that took shape in Nazism was not special to the Nazis during the years 1933 to 1945. Theirs was the most well organized and murderous. But the Germans did not slaughter six million Jews without the aid of hundreds of thousands who were not Germans.

That hatred is not dead. It lives in unknown numbers of people around the world today. It cuts across barriers and includes young and old, males and females, teenagers and college professors, rich and poor, the educated and uneducated.

A few governments express hostility toward Israel as the Jewish state, and at Jews in general. They secretly support terrorists who train in destruction and bloodshed even if it will mean they will lose their own lives. Most of these are in the Middle East. America is a prime target—as proven by the suicide attacks on the World Trade Center in New York City and on the Pentagon in Washington, D.C.

The actions of hate groups in the Western world regularly appear in the newspapers and on television.

At the extreme, some groups call themselves Nazis. They admire Hitler and the Third Reich, praise Hitler as the savior of the "Aryan" race (if only Germany had not lost the war), and call the Third Reich the ideal form of a pure and strong nation.

Others call themselves "skinheads." Usually these are young men who have shaved their heads to the skin—the reason for their name—and wear racist and Nazi tattoos. There are women among them who may or may not have shaved heads.

Skinheads are always white. They do not consider Jews to be white. They may call themselves "white supremacists" and demand "White Power." Many are drawn to violence.

Some groups aim their hatred exclusively at Jews. But most, like the original Nazis, are positively "democratic" in one way.

Surely they hate Jews. But just as much as they hate Jews, they also hate homosexuals, blacks, Chinese, Puerto Ricans, Koreans, Japanese, Mexicans, Arabs, foreigners in general and immigrants from almost any country. In short, they hate almost anyone who seems different from themselves.

Here are some examples of recent hate crimes. A few are not actually crimes, but they show the influence of the Nazi legacy in other ways. This list is short; a list of all hate crimes would be almost endless.

In Texas James Byrd Jr., a black man, is dragged to his death behind a pick-up truck driven by two white men, both members of a white supremacist organization.

In Wyoming a young homosexual named Matthew Shepard is tied to a fence, beaten and left to die because of his homosexuality. At his funeral, protesters carry signs that read GOD HATES FAGS or MATT IN HELL.

In New York a teenager covered with eighteen tattoos, including swastikas and white supremacist symbols, admits attacking two laborers because they are Mexican.

In Austria the leader of a popular political party has declared: "An orderly employment policy was carried out in the Third Reich." He refers to Mauthausen as a "punishment camp." At a reunion of former Waffen SS men, he says its members remind him that "in this world there are decent people who have character and have stuck to their beliefs . . . until today."

In Germany two sixteen-year-old males and their twenty-four-year-old friend attack an African immigrant, who dies three days later. They admit to membership in a neo-Nazi group.

In Illinois the black former basketball coach at Northwestern University is killed, six Orthodox Jews wounded, and two Asian-Americans are shot at in drive-by shootings.

In Italy during Mardi Gras, a float appears with a nearly full-size model of the entrance to Birkenau, including the sign ARBEIT MACHT FREI. Revelers wear striped concentration-camp uniforms.

In Russia a member of the government announces, "All the Yids [Jews] should be in graves." A newspaper headline blares, "It's time to drive all the Jews from Russia." Painted on the entrance to a Moscow Jewish cemetery is DEATH TO JEWS!

In Argentina the Israeli Embassy in Buenos Aires is bombed, killing 29 people, Jews and non-Jews. Two years later in the same city, the Jewish Community Building is destroyed, killing 86. Those responsible have never been found.

In Vermont a homosexual finds EXACUTE THE FAG! written across his fence ("execute" misspelled). A candidate for governor is greeted with a shouted "Watch out! The Jewish media is everywhere!" She does not respond to the comment, not even to say that it is completely untrue.

In Pittsburgh an attorney goes on a two-hour killing spree, starting with his Jewish neighbor. He paints swastikas on two synagogues and shoots out the windows. He also kills four Asians, proclaiming the rights and supremacy of white European Americans.

In Beirut, Lebanon, Arabs are asked in a survey of public opinion if they feel any sympathy with Jewish victims of the Holocaust. Eighty-two percent say no; 53 percent of that number say the Holocaust never occurred; and 32 percent say the Jews had plotted against Germany.

In Austria and Germany neo-Nazi computer games circulate widely. One of the most popular is "Concentration Camp Manager." The goal is to run the camp efficiently and send as many people as possible to the gas chambers.

In Germany four young men chase a Turkish worker, trample him with steel-tipped boots, and carve a two-inch swastika and the word *Death* across his scalp with a pocketknife.

Mein Kampf, Hitler's autobiography, is available on the Internet in English and in German. *The Protocols of the Elders of Zion,* the proven forgery the Nazis believed revealed Jewish plans to take over the world, is also available. Both can also be found in Arabic and other languages. As regular books, they continue to sell well in the United States and elsewhere. *The Protocols* has been used as a textbook in some schools in the Middle East.

In Los Angeles a member of an openly racist organization walks into a Jewish day-care center and opens fire, injuring five people, including three small boys and a teenage girl. Later the same day he shoots and kills a Filipino-American postal worker. The shooter says he intended the attack on the day-care center "to be a wake-up call to America to kill Jews."

THE INTERNET

The computer and the Internet have created a world without boundaries. Hate groups make good use of that opening to the rest of the world. It is estimated that there are over two thousand hate sites on the Internet, with more appearing almost daily.

The excerpts that follow are direct quotations from several of these sites. They are printed here exactly as they appear, mistakes in spelling, grammar, punctuation, capitalization intact.

The word *Aryan* is used to mean Christian white people, or whites from a Christian background.

The names of the sites are not given here. Any reader with a computer and an Internet connection can find them easily. Those without a computer should understand that the quotations are accurate.

"The blood of innocents was shed [at the World Trade Center and the Pentagon] because this government has America's nose in business . . . which benefits the Jews and no others."

"...the people who sat in darkness have seen a great light, and for those who sat in the region and shadow of death light has spawned."

MATTHEW 4:16

WEBSITE BERLIN

"...das Volk, das in Finsternis saß, hat ein Licht gesehen; und die da saßen am Ort und Schatten des Todes, denen ist ein Licht aufgegangen."

Hitler as savior. On the Internet today.

"HITLER WAS RIGHT! . . . This most extraordinary figure of modern times was right . . . when he raised the banner of Aryan truth against alien corruption and lies. . . . His message of racial idealism is every bit as relevant today as when it was first announced."

"All the homosexuals, race-mixers and hard-case collaborators in the country who are too far gone to be re-educated can be rounded up, packed into 10,000 or so cattle cars, and eventually double-timed into an abandoned coal mine in a few days' time."

An old print of black slaves and their white owners shows that "the plantation is . . . a happy and humane place where the slaves and slave owners are seen together, indicating a trust . . . between slave and owners . . . [and] indicating the likelihood that each slave would be treated humanely and respectfully."

"Whites are to jews as blacks are to whites. Jews evolved faster than whites because they weren't restrained by the same christian values expected from whites (besides that they eat their own)."

"We believe in the philosophies of Adolf Hitler and Nazi Germany. We believe the jews are trying to take over our country . . . We are dedicated to tell the White race that they must be stopped . . . Are enemies are the jews and the minorities."

"Most Jews are racist. Most chinks are racist. Most mestizos are racists. Most vietnamese are racist. Russian jews are racist. Our . . . injuns are racist . . . [But] they do not want Aryans to be racist."

"You were warned [before September 11, 2001] that by allowing the organized Jewish minority to control your media and government you would bring the hatred of many oppressed peoples upon you."

"Is it easy to win the battle for racial survival? No! But you can be sure that our jew and mud enemies are MAKING THE TIME to defeat US!!!"

"We support the unity of our movement and the revolutionizing of our spirit into a combined force to take back control of our Race's destiny, by any means necessary."

The winner of a skinhead tattoo contest. The cross on the chest of the man to the left is meant to show the martyrdom of the white race.

HOLOCAUST DENIAL

Many survivors of the Holocaust remember being told by the SS:

"However this war may end, we have won the war against you; . . . and even if some proof should remain and some of you survive, people will say the events you describe are too monstrous to be believed; they will say they are the exaggerations of . . . propaganda."

Holocaust denial works to make the prediction come true.

How can anyone deny the existence of something for which there is hard cold evidence? How can something be denied when there are witnesses who lived through the events? How can it be denied when those who carried it out admit what they have done?

The deniers say there is "another side" to the history of the Holocaust. What "other side"? The Holocaust happened. Six million Jews were murdered. There is no "other side."

Those who deny the Holocaust may be extremists, openly racist, ferociously anti-Semitic. But often they come clothed in the look of respectability and the appearance of scholarship. They present themselves as historians. They do not call their argument denial, and they do not call themselves deniers. They have named themselves "revisionists." They call their version of events "revisionism," as though they had revised and corrected facts that had been accepted as true—until they came along.

It must be said that serious and respected historians continually reexamine historical events. Such study can lead to the discovery of new facts and interpretations. In turn, they can bring about a new understanding of older interpretations and lead to a revision of the facts. That is true revisionism. It is how knowledge of the world grows.

But those who call themselves Holocaust revisionists deny accepted facts and manufacture new ones. They do it to advance their own views, not to increase knowledge. The so-called evidence they offer is twisted to their purpose, taken from unreliable or discredited sources or made up and simply untrue.

They have written books and articles, and they too make use of the Internet. Perhaps the largest and most effective of the revisionist groups publishes a scholarly journal. Full of figures, footnotes and long quotations, their writings claim to "reveal" the "true facts" about the Holocaust. They insist that the Holocaust never happened. At most, they might admit that large numbers of Jews died. But not six million, and not because of some plan for their extermination.

The appearance of respectable scholarship can be persuasive. It is not hard to believe them. As survivors and other witnesses die with time, people who know little about the Holocaust become more open to revisionist lies and half-truths. It is not easy to learn the facts that destroy their claims, and sometimes the facts are very complicated.

Revisionists have challenged historians who say they lie; the revisionists have not met the measure of facts. A well-known revisionist sued a major historian of the Holocaust for libel; he lost the case.

The revisionists offered a reward for "proof" that Jews were gassed at Auschwitz; given the proof, they did not want to pay up, were sued and settled out of court—with an apology.

A memo from Himmler to Hitler. Line 2C lists 363,211 Jews killed in the Soviet Union.

They write letters to the editors and run ads, especially in college newspapers and magazines in order to influence young people. They are smart enough to know that they cannot always convince. But they can create doubt. In this way they have been all too successful.

The Holocaust is so hideous and terrible, it would be a relief to think that it never happened. But it did. Men and women, like the men and women they killed, made it happen. That is the undeniable truth.

The remainder of this section will present several revisionist claims and the replies—the facts—that disprove those claims.

The same information, including entire revisionist publications, is widely available on the Internet. Libraries and bookstores also stock the material; it is easy enough to find.

The revisionists: It is not possible to have gassed six million people to death in such a short amount of time.
THE FACTS: This is correct. At their height, the gas chambers killed up to 20,000 Jews each day. The total number gassed is estimated to have been a maximum of only three million. But the gas chambers were not the only way Nazis killed Jews.

The Special Action Groups shot two million Jews throughout Eastern Europe. Mobile killing vans gassed an unknown number with diesel fumes in towns and villages. Others died in the ghettos. Still others died in random murders, and of starvation, disease, torture and killing "work" in so-called labor camps. The gas chambers took care of the rest.

The revisionists: There is no proof that Hitler ordered the extermination of the Jews. Such a huge undertaking could not even have begun without his express order, and no proof of such an order exists. Furthermore, there was no plan to exterminate the Jews.
THE FACTS: This is partly correct.

Probably there was no complete plan in the early years of Nazi power. Just as possibly, events as the war went on determined the steps of the Holocaust. But see chapter 5, "The Final Solution." The Wannsee Conference in 1942 produced the complete plan to exterminate the Jews of Europe.

As for the rest of the revisionist claim: Yes, it is true that no written order from Hitler has been found.

But Hitler often did not put his most important orders in writing. He gave them orally. Himmler, Eichmann, Heydrich and others have all said that the orders for the annihilation of the Jews came directly from Hitler. There is ample evidence that these Nazis and others acted in obedience to what was called a *Führerbefel*—a Hitler order, or expressed as *Führerwünscht*—Hitler wishes. Such an order was not to be questioned.

Hitler revealed his intention of murdering the Jews before he came to power and after. It is there in his autobiography, *Mein Kampf,* quoted in this book's chapter 1.

In 1939 he gave a speech in which he said if there was war, the result would be "the annihilation of the Jews of Europe"; it is quoted at the start of chapter 3.

In 1944 Goebbels quoted him as saying, "There is nothing else open to modern peoples than to exterminate the Jews."

But even long before then, he made his wishes plain. In 1922 he said:

"Once I really am in power, my first and foremost task will be the annihilation of the Jews. As soon as I have the power to do so, I will have gallows built in rows—at the Marienplatz [a major thoroughfare] in Munich, for example—as many as traffic allows.

"Then the Jews will be hanged indiscriminately, and they will remain hanging there . . . as long as the principles of hygiene permit. As soon as they have been untied, the next batch will be strung up, until the last Jew in Munich has been exterminated. Other cities will follow suit, precisely in this fashion, until all Germany has been completely cleansed of Jews."

Hitler's hatred of Jews was bone-deep. As the ruler of Germany, his power was almost complete. It is just not logical to believe that the Holocaust could have happened without his wanting it to happen, and without his order to make it happen.

The revisionists: Hitler did not want to murder the Jews. He only wanted them to leave Germany and Europe and go somewhere else.
THE FACTS: See the reply to the previous claim. Hitler's own words prove this to be false.

One small kernel of this revisionist claim is true. During their early years in power, the Nazis wanted Jews out of Germany. Over 300,000 did leave. But when German conquests in other parts of Europe brought more and more Jews under Nazi control, getting them to leave became no longer practical. Instead, the Nazis brought Jews from all over Europe and concentrated them in ghettos. The Special Action Groups and Order Police killed those they found outside the ghettos.

From there, as the notes of the Wannsee Conference make clear, the next step was to get rid of the Jews entirely—by killing them.

The revisionists: Germany needed all the manpower it could find during the war. Killing off such a huge labor force does not make sense.
THE FACTS: No, it makes no sense. That is correct. Even some Nazis, though not of the highest ranks, thought that. But one of the major aims of the war was the extermination of the Jews. That way it does make sense.

The revisionists: The figure of six million was concocted by the Jews in order to "blackmail" Germany into paying enough to finance the state of Israel.
THE FACTS: False on both counts.

First, the basic facts about the Holocaust were established before Israel was founded in 1948.

Second, the amount of money Germany paid to Israel after the war was not based on the number of Jews killed. It was based on two things that were exactly the opposite of that. One, on the number of Jews who had escaped Nazi-dominated Europe and had already come to Israel. Two, on those survivors that Israel expected to settle there after the war. The estimate: 500,000 Jews. Not six million.

Furthermore, if the figure of six million was only a "Jewish lie" to get money, why was it set so high? A smaller number—two million, say, or even three or four million—would have meant more Jews left alive and even more money for Israel.

The revisionists deny both the truth and plain common sense.

The revisionists: The documents that are used as evidence of Nazi crimes and proof of the Holocaust are forgeries. They were made during the war and planted then or immediately after the war, probably by Jews.

THE FACTS: Captured Nazi documents are in archives in Germany, the United States, France, Russia, Poland, Great Britain and other countries. In every archive, there are documents that refer to the murder of the Jews.

It is almost unimaginable that great numbers of people worked during the war and after to create these forgeries. It is completely unimaginable that any unseen group managed to find a way to plant the forgeries where they would be found by the victors—and not be noticed while they did so.

And what about entries in Goebbels' personal diary? One entry is quoted at the opening of chapter 7. A speech by Hans Frank is quoted at the beginning of chapter 5. Himmler's speech to the SS is quoted at the start of chapter 9; the magnetic-tape recording made at his order lies in the National Archives in Washington, D.C.

Proof of the mass murder of Jews lies in the Nazis' own words, written and spoken. Denial is a lie.

The revisionists: Nazi confessions made during the Nuremberg Trials prove nothing. They were made because the defendants were tortured into making them.

THE FACTS: There is not one shred of evidence for this. Shaken by what they had seen, perhaps a few Allied soldiers roughed up some Nazis. But torture? No. The revisionists offer a few sources for this claim, but none—none at all—holds up under investigation.

The revisionists say that the Nuremberg confessions are especially suspicious because the trials were held in an international court, and the court was made up of the winners of the war.

Even if those particular confessions came through torture—which they did not—what about the confessions at later trials? Those took place in Germany under German law, in German courts, before German judges. The confessions were of murder and worse than murder. Did the Germans torture their own to make themselves look bad?

The revisionists: The gas chambers at Auschwitz were built by the British for the Poles to use as a tourist attraction after the war.

THE FACTS: The gas chambers, along with much else in Auschwitz, were completely destroyed by the Nazis as the Russians advanced toward the camp. The Germans left as little evidence behind them as they could.

The gas chambers, undressing rooms and crematoriums at the Auschwitz camp site today are reconstructions. The structures were rebuilt according to original German documents, including blueprints, used by the Nazis to build the camp in the first place and later to expand it. That evidence the Nazis neglected to destroy.

The guides at the camp today tell visitors that the gas chambers and much else are reconstructions; they do not lie.

The revisionists: The photographs of piles of bodies that circulated around the world after the war are faked. Or else they could be the bodies of Germans killed by Allied bombings, or the corpses of those dead of disease. They were moved into place in order to take the photographs. The captions could then say anything at all.

THE FACTS: It is possible to fake any photograph. True. But by now, with all the advanced technology available, surely some proof of the faking would have been discovered. None has been found.

The bodies of bombing victims would show signs of physical damage—missing limbs, for example, and wounds of all sorts. Almost none of the corpses in the photographs show any such signs.

The bodies were emaciated—of people starved almost into skeletons. The German people suffered many hardships during the war, but they did not starve. Nor would any disease have left so many dead in that condition.

Thousands of witnesses, not only from the Allies but also from among the Germans, do not question the reality of those stacks of starved corpses. The photographs are not faked.

The revisionists: Six million Jews were not killed. They were still in Europe at the end of the war, except for a few hundred thousand.

THE FACTS: They are not there now, and they were not there at the end of the war. Where are they? Where did they go? There has been no flood of millions of Jews to any country or spread out over several countries that would explain the missing millions.

Six million Jews cannot be accounted for—except by the Holocaust.

The revisionists: The Nazis did not use poison gas to kill Jews. Zyklon B, the gas said to have been used to kill Jewish millions, would have left large traces behind on the walls of the gas chambers. Such traces would still be detectable today. Investigation has found only tiny or no amounts at all. That proves the chambers could not have been used to kill masses of people, especially hour after hour and day after day.

THE FACTS: This is the center of revisionist belief that the Holocaust is a lie. It is found in *The Leuchter Report: An Engineering Report on the Alleged Execution Chambers at Auschwitz, Birkenau, and Majdanek, Poland.*

Here is the truth.

The "investigation" was carried out by Fred Leuchter, a man with no scientific or engineering training whatever.

Without permission, Leuchter took stone and brick samples from several camp crematoriums, especially Auschwitz. He had himself videotaped as he did so. With hammer and chisel, he knocked out chunks of brick and stone. The pieces were sent to an independent lab for analysis, where they were smashed into powder for the tests. They showed no trace of Zyklon B. Therefore, concluded Leuchter, Jews were not killed by poison gas.

But here is a crucial fact: smashed into powder, the stone would show no traces of the gas. Leuchter did not know that Zyklon B penetrates to less than the depth of a human hair. He had asked for the wrong test.

He continues to be wrong. The gas chambers were not used on a twenty-four-hour daily basis. The Nazis found they could not burn the bodies fast enough, among other reasons. The gas chambers went unused when too many Jews were killed to remove their bodies quickly enough to keep the area "clean."

Furthermore, the Nazis blew up the gas chambers before they left. The stone and bricks have been lying exposed to the elements since 1945. Weather and time alone would have removed small traces of the gas.

Leuchter goes on: The rooms used to delouse clothes contain larger traces of Zyklon B than the so-called gas chambers.

That is correct. But it takes much greater amounts of Zyklon B to kill lice than it does to kill humans. It also takes more time—up to eighteen hours for infested clothes. Humans absorb the poison through their lungs and die within minutes, with much smaller amounts of the gas.

The Nazis did not blow up the delousing chambers. The rooms remain in one piece. Their thick walls and ceiling have protected them from the wearing-away of time and weather. The ruined rubble of the gas chambers has no such protection.

Leuchter's "evidence" and reasoning go into far greater detail than this. But his "facts" and denial are false. Scientific and well-informed investigation prove the lie of his conclusions.

An extensive correctly conducted analysis was carried out with samples from the same sites in 1994 by the Institute for Forensic Research in Cracow, Poland. Zyklon B was found in almost all samples.

Leuchter and many deniers continue to use Leuchter's evidence and arguments to "prove" that Jews were not gassed. None of the evidence is scientifically based, and all of the arguments are false.

Millions of Jews were killed in the gas chambers—and elsewhere—of the Third Reich. There is no argument.

Is there any reason to go on with this? The revisionists' claims can all be disproved, one by one. To put it plainly, they are not true.

The claims and rebuttals and much other material from "both sides" can be found on the Internet; a few of those sites are given in the Partial List of Sources beginning on page 231. Dozens of Internet links connect with original documents from before, during and after the war; with Nazi material; with revisionist material; with Allied records and trial transcripts; and much more. Any interested reader can go on from there.

THE MESSAGE

No. It is not time to sit back and relax.

The hate groups and Holocaust deniers must be taken seriously. Their number grows steadily larger and their actions become ever more dangerous.

It does not matter if someone is not a Jew, not a black, not homosexual, not Mexican or Puerto Rican, an Asian or Arab or a foreigner. No one is safe from hate.

A German Protestant pastor, Martin Niemoller, spoke up for the Jews.

A desecrated Jewish cemetery.

He spent almost nine years in a concentration camp for his courage. This is what he said:

"The Nazis came for the Communists, and I didn't speak up because I wasn't a Communist. Then they came for the Jews, and I didn't speak up because I wasn't a Jew. Then they came for the trade unionists, and I didn't speak up because I wasn't a trade unionist. Then they came for the Catholics, and I didn't speak up because I was a Protestant. Then they came for me, and by that time there was no one left to speak for me."

A survivor put it in simpler words:

"All that it takes for evil to triumph is for the good to do nothing."

That is the message of this chapter, and that is the message of the Holocaust.

PARTIAL LIST OF SOURCES

Eyewitness Accounts

Adelson, Alan, and Robert Lapides, comp. and ed. *Lodz Ghetto: Inside a Community Under Siege.* New York: Viking Penguin, 1989.

Berg, Mary. *Warsaw Ghetto: A Diary.* New York: L. B. Fisher, 1945.

Delbo, Charlotte. *Auschwitz and After.* New Haven, Conn., and London: Yale University Press, 1995. Paper.

Donat, Alexander. *The Holocaust Kingdom: A Memoir.* New York: The Holocaust Library, 1963. Paper.

Frank, Anne. *The Diary of a Young Girl.* New York: Pocket Books, 1953. Paper.

Goebbels, Joseph. *Final Entries 1945: The Diaries of Joseph Goebbels.* Hugh Trevor-Roper, ed. New York: G. P. Putnam's Sons, 1978.

———. *The Goebbel Diaries 1942–1943.* Louis P. Lochner, ed. New York: Doubleday & Company, Inc., 1948.

Goldstein, Bernard. *The Stars Look Down.* New York: Viking, 1949.

Hart, Kitty. *Return to Auschwitz.* New York: Atheneum, 1985.

Heimler, Eugene. *Night of the Mist.* New York: Vanguard Press, 1959.

Hoess, Rudolf. Affidavit, International Military Tribunal, Cybary of the Holocaust. http://remember.org/Facts/aft.trl.nur.html

———. *Commandant of Auschwitz: Autobiography of Rudolf Hoess.* Cleveland: World Publishing, 1959.

Kogon, Eugen. *The Theory and Practice of Hell.* New York: Berkeley Books, 1960. Paper.

Lengyel, Olga. *Five Chimneys.* Chicago: Ziff-Davis, 1947.

Levi, Primo. *The Drowned and the Saved*. New York: Summit Books, a division of Simon & Schuster, 1988.

——. *Survival in Auschwitz*. New York: Collier Books, 1961. Paper.

Müller, Filip. *Eyewitness to Auschwitz*. New York: Stein & Day, 1979. Paper.

Newman, Judith. *In the Hell of Auschwitz*. New York: Exposition Press, 1966.

Nomberg-Przytk, Sara. *Auschwitz: True Tales from a Grotesque Land*. Chapel Hill, N.C.: University of North Carolina Press, 1985.

Stroop, Jürgen. *The Stroop Report: "The Jewish Quarter of Warsaw Is No More."* New York: Pantheon Books, a division of Random House, 1979. Unpaged. Paper.

Wiesel, Elie. *Night*. New York: Avon Books, 1972. Paper.

REFERENCES

Abzug, Robert H. *Inside the Vicious Heart*. New York and Oxford, England: Oxford University Press, 1985.

Arad, Yitzhak. *Belzec, Sobibor, Treblinka: The Operation Reinhard Death Camps*. Bloomington and Indianapolis: Indiana University Press, 1987.

Arad, Yitzhak, Shumel Krakowski and Shumel Spector, eds. *The Einsatzgruppen Reports: Selections from the Dispatches of the Nazi Death Squads' Campaign Against the Jews in the Occupied Territories of the Soviet Union July 1941–January 1943*. New York: The Holocaust Library, 1989. Paper.

Bartlett, John. Justin Kaplan, ed. *Familiar Quotations*, 16th ed. Boston: Little, Brown and Company, 1992.

Berenbaum, Michael, and Abraham J. Peck, eds. *The Holocaust and History: The Known, the Unknown, the Disputed, and the Reexamined*. Bloomington and Indianapolis: Indiana University Press, published in association with the United States Holocaust Memorial Museum, Washington, D.C., 1998.

Berkovits, Eliezer. *With God in Hell: Judaism in the Ghettos and Death Camps*. New York: Sanhedrin Press, 1979.

Bleuel, Hans Peter. *Sex and Society in Nazi Germany*. Philadelphia and New York: J. B. Lippincott Company, 1973.

Block, Gay, and Malka Drucker. *Rescuers: Portraits of Moral Courage in the Holocaust*. New York and London: Holmes and Meier Publishers, 1992.

Breitman, Richard. *Official Secrets: What the Nazis Planned, What the British and Americans Knew*. New York: Hill and Wang, 1998.

Browning, Christopher. *Ordinary Men: Reserve Police Battalion 101 and the Final Solution in Poland*. New York: HarperCollins Publishers, 1992. With new Afterword, Harper Perennial, 1998. Paper.

Clendinnen, Inga. *Reading the Holocaust*. Cambridge, England: Cambridge University Press, 1999.

Czech, Danuta. *Auschwitz Chronicle 1939–1945*. New York: Henry Holt and Company, 1990.

Dawidowicz, Lucy, ed. *A Holocaust Reader*. New York: Behrman House, 1976. Paper.

———. *The War Against the Jews: 1933–1945*. Tenth anniversary ed. New York: Seth Press, 1986.

Des Pres, Terrence. *The Survivor: An Anatomy of Life in the Death Camps*. New York and Oxford, England: Oxford University Press, 1976. Paper.

Dimensions of the Holocaust: Lectures at Northwestern University. Evanston, Illinois: Northwestern University, 1997.

Dumbach, Annette E., and Jud Newborn. *Shattering the German Night: The Story of the White Rose*. Boston: Little, Brown and Company, 1986.

Eliach, Yaffa. *Hasidic Tales of the Holocaust*. New York and Oxford, England: New York and Oxford University Press, 1982.

Facing History and Ourselves: Holocaust and Human Behavior. Resource Book. Brookline, Mass.: Facing History and Ourselves National Foundation, Inc., 1994.

Fischer, Klaus P. *The History of an Obsession: German Judeophobia and the Holocaust*. New York: Continuum Publishing Company, 1998.

———. *Nazi Germany: A New History*. New York: Continuum Publishing Company, 1995.

Fleming, Gerald. *Hitler and the Final Solution*. Berkeley and Los Angeles: University of California Press, 1982. Paper.

Frankl, Viktor. *From Death Camp to Existentialism*. Boston: Beacon Press, 1959.

Furet, Francois, ed. *Unanswered Questions: Nazi Germany and the Genocide of the Jews*. New York: Schocken Books, 1989.

Gilbert, Martin. *Atlas of the Holocaust*. London: Michael Joseph, 1982. Paper.

———. *Auschwitz and the Allies.* New York: Holt, Rinehart and Winston, 1981.

———. *The Holocaust: The History of the Jews of Europe During the Second World War.* New York: Holt, Rinehart and Winston, 1985.

Goldhagen, Daniel Jonah. *Hitler's Willing Executioners: Ordinary Germans and the Holocaust.* New York: Alfred A. Knopf, 1996.

Grobman, Alex, and Daniel Landes, eds. *Genocide: Critical Issues of the Holocaust.* Los Angeles and Chappaqua, N.Y.: Simon Wiesenthal Center and Rossel Books, 1983.

Gutman, Yisrael, and Michael Berenbaum, eds. *Anatomy of the Auschwitz Death Camp.* Bloomington and Indianapolis: Indiana University Press, published in association with the United States Holocaust Memorial Museum, Washington, D.C., 1998. Paper.

Haffner, Sebastian. *The Meaning of Hitler.* Cambridge: Harvard University Press, 1979.

Hamburg Institute for Social Research, ed. *The German Army and Genocide: Crimes Against War Prisoners, Jews, and Other Civilians in the East, 1939–1944.* New York: The New Press, 1999.

Hilberg, Raul. *The Destruction of the European Jews.* Rev. ed. 3 vols. New York: Holmes and Meier Publishers, 1985.

———, ed. *Documents of Destruction: Germany and Jewry 1933–1945.* Chicago: Quadrangle Books, 1976. Paper.

Hitler, Adolf. *Mein Kampf.* Boston: Houghton Mifflin, 1971. Paper.

———. *Mein Kampf.* Annotated ed. New York: Revnal & Hitchcock, 1940.

Jäckel, Eberhard. *Hitler's World View.* Cambridge: Harvard University Press, 1981. Paper.

Kaplan, Marion A. *Between Dignity and Despair: Jewish Life in Nazi Germany.* New York and Oxford, England: Oxford University Press, 1998. Paper.

Karski, Jan. *Story of a Secret State.* Boston: Houghton Mifflin, 1944.

Kershaw, Ian. *Hitler 1936–1945: Nemesis.* New York: W. W. Norton & Company, 2000.

Klee, Ernst, Willi Dressen, and Volker Riess, eds. *"The Good Old Days": The Holocaust as Seen by Its Perpetrators and Bystanders.* New York: Konecky & Konecky, 1991.

Laqueur, Walter. *The Terrible Secret: Suppression of the Truth About Hitler's "Final Solution."* New York: Henry Holt and Company, 1980; With a new Introduction by the author, Owl Books, 1998. Paper.

Lee, Martin A. *The Beast Reawakens.* New York: Routledge, 2000. Paper.

Lewy, Guenter. "Gypsies and Jews Under Hitler," *Holocaust and Genocide Studies* 13, no. 3 (Winter 1999): 383–404.

Lifton, Robert Jay. *The Nazi Doctors: Medical Killing and the Psychology of Genocide.* New York: Basic Books, 1986.

Lipstadt, Deborah. *Denying the Holocaust: The Growing Assault on Truth and Memory.* New York: Free Press, 1993.

Manvell, Roger, and Heinrich Fraenkel. *The Incomparable Crime: Mass Extermination in the Twentieth Century.* New York: G. P. Putnam's Sons, 1967.

Marrus, Michael R. *The Holocaust in History.* Hanover, N.H.: University Press of New England, 1987.

Mayer, Arno J. *Why Did the Heavens Not Darken? The "Final Solution" in History.* New York: Pantheon Books, a division of Random House, 1988.

Morse, Arthur D. *While Six Million Died: A Chronicle of American Apathy.* New York: Overlook Press, 1998. Paper.

Mosse, George L. *Nazi Culture: Intellectual, Cultural and Social Life in the Third Reich.* New York: Grosset and Dunlap, The Universal Library, 1966. Paper.

Noakes, J., and G. Pridham, eds. *Nazism 1919–1945: A Documentary Reader;* Vol. 2, *State, Economy and Society 1933–1939;* Vol. 3, *Foreign Policy, War and Racial Extermination.* Exeter, England: University of Exeter, 1984. Paper.

Poliakov, Leon. *Harvest of Hate.* Rev. ed. New York: The Holocaust Library, 1979. Paper.

Reitlinger, Gerald. *The SS: Alibi of a Nation 1922–1945.* London: Arms and Armour Press, 1981.

Remak, Joachim. *The Nazi Years: A Documentary History.* New York: Simon & Schuster, Touchstone Books, 1969. Paper.

Rittner, Carol, and Sondra Myers, eds. *The Courage to Care: Rescuers of Jews During the Holocaust.* New York: New York University Press, 1986.

Rozett, Robert, and Shmuel Spector. *Encyclopedia of the Holocaust.* Jerusalem, Israel: Yad Vashem and the Jerusalem Publishing House, co-published with Facts on File, New York, 2000.

Sachor, Abram S. *Redemption of the Unwanted: From the Liberation of the Death Camps to the Founding of Israel.* New York: St. Martin's Press, 1983.

Schoenberner, Gerhard. *The Yellow Star: The Persecution of the Jews in Europe 1933–1945.* New York: Bantam Books, 1973. Paper.

Sereny, Gitta. *Albert Speer: His Battle with Truth.* New York: Alfred A. Knopf, 1995.

———. *Into That Darkness: From Mercy Killing to Mass Murder.* New York: McGraw-Hill, 1974.

Shermer, Michael, and Alex Grobman, eds. *Denying History: Who Says the Holocaust Never Happened and Why Do They Say It?* Berkeley and Los Angeles: University of California Press, 2000.

Stoltzfus, Nathan. *Resistance of the Heart: Intermarriage and the Rosenstrasse Protest in Nazi Germany.* New York: W. W. Norton Company, 1997.

Suhl, Yuri, ed. *They Fought Back: The Story of Jewish Resistance in Nazi Europe.* New York: Schocken Books, 1975.

Tatelbaum, Itzhak B., ed. *Through Our Eyes: Children Witness the Holocaust.* Jerusalem, Israel: I.B.T. Publishing, 1985. Paper.

Wistrich, Robert S. *Who Was Who in Nazi Germany.* New York and London: Routledge, 1995. Paper.

Wyman, David S. *The Abandonment of the Jews.* New York: Pantheon Books, 1984. Paper.

Yad Vashem. *Jewish Resistance During the Holocaust.* Proceedings of the Conference on Manifestations of Jewish Resistance. Jerusalem, Israel: Yad Vashem, 1971.

———. *The Nazi Concentration Camps.* Proceedings of the Fourth Yad Vashem Historical Conference, January 1980. Jerusalem, Israel: Yad Vashem, 1984.

INTERNET SITES

BBC News History Files, Yugoslavia and the Balkans 1900–1988
    http://news.bbc.co.uk./hi/english/yugoslavia
Human Rights Watch
    http://www.hrw.org/reports/1999/Rwanda
International Criminal Tribunal for the Former Yugoslavia
    http://www.un.org/icty/index.html
International Criminal Tribunal for Rwanda
    http://www.ictr.org
International Military Tribunal: Nuremberg War Crime Trials
    http://www.yale.edu/lawweb/avalon/imt/imt.htm
Research in Review, Fall/Winter 1997
    http://research/fsu.edu/ResearchR/
    fallwinter97/features/hitler.html

In addition to the historical information on the sites that follow, their links
lead to a large variety of different kinds of material: original documents in both
English and German, essays and discussions by scholars and historians, denial
and hate sites, time lines and histories, and photographs taken at the time.

Anti-Defamation League
    http://www.adl.org
Cybary of the Holocaust
    http://remember.org.html
Hate Watch
    www.hatewatch.org
Nizkor: Your Holocaust Educational Resource
    http://www.nizkor.com
Simon Wiesenthal Center
    http://www.wiesenthal.com
United States Holocaust Memorial Museum
    http:www.ushmm.org
Yad Vashem
    http://www.yad-vashem.org

SOURCE NOTES FOR THE QUOTATIONS

Note to the Reader: The first edition of *Smoke and Ashes* was researched and written approximately fifteen years ago. Over that time, some source information has been lost or misplaced. Incomplete or missing sources will be completed and added as they are found and will appear in future editions.

The first time a source appears, the author's last name and the title of the book are given. The author's last name is used throughout, but only key words of the title appear after its first mention. Most references are to titles cited in the Partial List of Sources.

1. THE ROOTS

1	"Their synagogues," Grobman and Landes, *Genocide*, p. 84.
1	"When Jewish blood," Morse, *While Six Million Died*, p. 105.
3	"Death and destruction," Dawidowicz, *War Against the Jews*, p. 30.
4	"the liberation," Dawidowicz, *Holocaust Reader*, pp. 28–29.
4	"The Jews are indeed," Dawidowicz, *War*, p. 41.
5	"Only a racial comrade," Remak, *Nazi Years*, p. 28.
9	All quotations from Hitler, *Mein Kampf*, throughout.

2. THE NAZIS AND THE JEWS OF GERMANY

10	"We love," Remak, *Nazi Years*, p. 69.
10	"Hatred," Fleming, *Hitler and the Final Solution*, p. 15.
11	"Hitler, you're our man," Remak, *Nazi Years*, p. 126.
15	"I will ruthlessly," Dawidowicz, *War*, p. 52.
16	"Perhaps the foreign," Goebbels, March 26, 1933.*

* The Goebbels quotations in this book come from several different histories of the period and are translations from the original German as used by the authors. The wording may differ from translation to translation, but the meaning remains the same. However, the dates of the entries do not change. They are relatively easy to find whatever source is used. Translations of two volumes of the diaries appear in the Partial List of Sources.

17–18   "The age of extreme," Noakes and Pridham, *Nazism*, vol. 2, pp. 401–2.

23   "At very short notice," Schoenberner, *Yellow Star*, p. 20.

23   "Such measures," to come.

24   "All the Jewish," Schoenberner, *Yellow Star*, p. 21.

24   "I would not like," Fischer, *History of an Obsession*, p. 286.

3. THE GHETTOS

28   "Today I am going," Jäckel, *Hitler's World View*, p. 61.

33–34   "The creation of the ghetto," Noakes and Pridham, *Nazism*, vol. 3, p. 1063.

34   caption: "who are dying," Noakes and Pridham, *Nazism*, vol. 3, p. 1067.

37   "Starvation was the lament," Schoenberner, *Yellow Star*, p. 67.

37   "In the early morning," Fischer, *Obsession*, p. 321.

39   "I am hungry," to come.

40   "These were still," Karski, *Story of a Secret State*, p. 330.

41–42   "On December 1," Noakes and Pridham, *Nazism*, vol. 3, p. 1071.

42–43   "Once when I was walking," Tatelbaum, *Through Our Eyes*, p. 72.

43   "The evacuation," Mayer, *Why Did the Heavens Not Darken?* p. 304.

4. SPECIAL ACTION GROUPS AND THEIR HELPERS

44   "I can state," Klee, *"The Good Old Days,"* p. 193.

44   "This is a glorious," Kershaw, *Hitler 1936–1945*, pp. 604–5.

44   "would enter a village," Manvell and Fraenkel, *Incomparable Crime*, pp. 114–15.

44–45   "Men from fourteen," Dawidowicz, *War*, p. 128.

45–46   "The Jews," Gilbert, *Holocaust*, p. 235.

47   "The execution," Schoenberner, *Yellow Star*, p. 111.

48   "I must admit," Goldhagen, *Hitler's Willing Executioners*, p. 452.

48   "The actions," Reitlinger, *The SS*, p. 127.
50   "From the first day," Noakes and Pridham, *Nazism*, vol. 3, p. 1095.
50   "So far," Goldhagen, *Willing Executioners*, p. 404.
51   "The shooting squads," Hamburg Institute, *The German Army and Genocide*, p. 60.
51–52   "as they did in Kovno," Fischer, *Nazi Germany*, p. 501.
52   "All Jews," Shermer and Grobman, *Denying History*, p.191.
52   "[It would be] impossible," Fischer, *Nazi Germany*, p. 503.

5. THE FINAL SOLUTION

55   "We cannot," Gilbert, *Holocaust*, p. 106.
56   "I herewith," Schoenberner, *Yellow Star*, p. 132.
58–59   "These gentlemen," *Encyclopedia of the Holocaust*, vol. 2, p. 657.
59   "after this Wannsee conference," Lipstadt, *Denying the Holocaust*, p. 199.
59   "Within the framework," Fischer, *Obsession*, p. 133.

6. OTHER VICTIMS

61   "The law," Fleming, *Hitler*, p. 27.
63   "should be removed," Gutman and Berenbaum, *Anatomy of the Auschwitz Death Camp*, p. 417.
64   "a symptom of degeneracy," Bleuel, *Sex and Society in Nazi Germany*, p. 222.
65   "simple arithmetic," Haffner, *Meaning of Hitler*, p. 134.

7. DEPORTATIONS

68   "Not much," Goebbels, *Diaries*, March 27, 1942.
68   "On August 11," Gilbert, *Holocaust*, pp. 319–20.
71   "The forces," "A large number," "It is recommended," Poliakov, *Harvest of Hate*, p. 127.
71   "The spectacle," Gilbert, *Holocaust*, p. 320.
73   "What makes you," Dawidowicz, *War*, p. 304.

| 75 | "The important thing," Schoenberner, *Yellow Star,* p. 168. |
| 77 | "With particular joy," Hilberg, *Destruction of the European Jews,* p. 491. |

8. THE CAMPS

78	"I am of the opinion," Schoenberner, *Yellow Star,* p. 191.
78	"The wagon doors," Des Pres, *Survivor,* p. 77.
78	"We had two," Affidavit of Rudolf Hoess, International Military Tribunal, Cybary of the Holocaust, http://remember.org/Facts/aft.trl.nur.html.
78–79	"I had the opportunity," Tatelbaum, *Our Eyes,* p. 102.
80	"Corpses," Newman, *In the Hell of Auschwitz,* p. 18.
81	"Just as," Levi, *Survival in Auschwitz,* p. 112.
82	"Comrades," Fischer, *Nazi Germany,* p. 229.
87–88	"What, really, is the difference," Des Pres, *Survivor,* p. 114.
91	"On behalf," Müller, *Eyewitness to Auschwitz,* pp. 80–81.
92	"When the last," Müller, *Eyewitness to Auschwitz,* p. 38.
94	"most of the clothing," Schoenberner, *Yellow Star,* p. 75.
94	"The riches," Remak, *Nazi Years,* p. 159.

9. LIFE IN THE CAMPS

95	"We were forced," Manvell, *Incomparable,* p. 44.
95	"had set out to break our morale," Frankl, *From Death Camp to Existentialism,* p. 13.
96	"We really had nothing," Frankl, *From Death Camp,* p. 13.
97	"From now on," Tatelbaum, *Our Eyes,* p. 97.
97	"In a moment," Levi, *Survival,* p. 22.
97	"A prisoner," Yad Vashem, *Nazi Concentration Camps,* p. 35.
101	"A fortnight," Levi, *Survival,* to come.
103	"He believed," Fischer, *Nazi Germany,* p. 516.
103	"The most important," Hart, *Return to Auschwitz,* p. 63.
104	"Help one another," Wiesel, *Night,* p. 55.
104	"Here there are," Wiesel, *Night,* p. 122.

105   "It seems odd," Nomberg-Pryztk, *Auschwitz*, p. 98.

105   "There were things," Heimler, *Night of the Mist*, p. 191.

105   "Some of us," Hart, *Return*, p. 95.

10. FIGHTING BACK

106   "Listen," Berkovits, *With God in Hell*, p. 110.

106   "I don't know," Eliach, *Hasidic Tales of the Holocaust*, p. 105.

110   "Why talk about," Tatelbaum, *Our Eyes*, p. 129.

111   "315 Jewish men," "864 Jewish men," Hilberg, *Documents of Destruction*, p. 53.

113   "The Nazis demanded," Grobman and Landes, *Genocide*, p. 169.

114   "Our entire existence was marked," Clendinnen, *Reading the Holocaust*, p. 57, "We revisited," p. 11.

115   "All of a sudden," Müller, *Eyewitness*, p. 87.

115–116 "The SS men," Nomberg-Przytk, *Auschwitz*, p. 108.

116   "I decided," Arad, *Belzec, Sobibor, Treblinka*, p. 217.

11. ARMED RESISTANCE

121   "The last wish," Grobman and Landes, *Genocide*, p. 193.

122   "If we are too weak," Yad Vashem, *Jewish Resistance During the Holocaust*, p. 317.

123   "One sees," Goebbels, *Diaries*, May 1, 1943.

125   "The public wants," Yad Vashem, *Resistance*, p. 313.

125   "The merest German private," Dawidowicz, *War*, p. 274.

125   "We have nothing," "I am not so sure," Dawidowicz, *War*, p. 330.

126   "I have no power," Dawidowicz, *Reader*, p. 374.

128   "The roundups," to come.

130   "We were happy," Dawidowicz, *War*, p. 337.

130   "The rejoicing," Gilbert, *Holocaust*, p. 558.

131   "We danced," Suhl, *They Fought Back*, to come.

131   "One saw," Stroop, *Stroop Report*, May 24, 1943.

131   "The only method," Stroop, April 26, 1943.

131   "The Jewish quarter," Stroop, April 30, 1944.

131   "Inherently," "bandits," Stroop, throughout.
135   "Comrades," Arad, *Belzec*, p. 330.
141   "If there is any purpose," Goldstein, *The Stars Look Down*, p. 275.

12. THE COMING END

142   "I gave," Fischer, *Obsession*, p. 146.
143   "Every day," Gilbert, *Holocaust*, p. 585.
143   "We dug," "Among those," Gilbert, *Holocaust*, p. 669.
146   "On the death march," Gilbert, *Holocaust*, p. 774.
146   "If I were asked," Goldhagen, *Executioners*, p. 371.

13. THE UNITED STATES AND GREAT BRITAIN

147   "If horses," Wyman, *Abandonment of the Jews*, p. 94.
147   "In my opinion," Gilbert, *Auschwitz and the Allies*, p. 312.
148–149   Surveys, Marrus, *Holocaust in History*, p. 162.
149   "As we have," Morse, *Six Million*, p. 212.
150   "I could scarcely," Morse, *Six Million*, p. 231.
152   "Received alarming report," Laqueur, *Terrible Secret*, p. 77.
154   "The positive solution," Gilbert, *Auschwitz*, p. 328.
155   "without foundation," "create confusion," to come.
155–156   "If we do that," "concerned with the difficulties," "lead to an offer,"
          "likely to bring," "So far as I know," "take the burden," to come.
157   "We have no option," Gilbert, *Auschwitz*, p. 306.
158   "After a study," Wyman, *Abandonment*, to come.
159   "The fact that," Breitman, *Official Secrets*, p. 96.
159–160   "If there had," Breitman, *Secrets*, p. 191.
161   "One of the greatest crimes," Wyman, *Abandonment*, p. 296.
161   "for the rescue," to come.
162   "In one of the blackest," Morse, *Six Million*, p. 337.

14. THE RESCUERS AND THE RIGHTEOUS

163   "I think you," Rittner and Myers, *The Courage to Care*, p. 29.

166–179   Quotations from several of the Righteous come from various sources, including Rittner and Myers, *Courage;* Block and Drucker, *Rescuers;* and various sites on the Internet devoted to the Righteous Among the Nations, especially Yad Vashem.

167   "I have indeed," "Here we all are," Sachor, *Redemption of the Unwanted,* p. 91.

175–178   Dumbach and Newborn, *Shattering the German Night,* throughout.

179   "There have been," Goebbels, *Diaries,* March 6, 1943.

179   "Goebbels released," Ash, "The Day Hitler Blinked," Research in Review, Fall/Winter 1997. http://research/fsu.edu/ResearchR/fallwinter97/features97/hitler.html

15. IS THE HOLOCAUST UNIQUE?

182   "We are mad," Bartlett, *Familiar Quotations,* p. 102.

188   "Never before had," Jäckel, *Hitler's World View,* to come.

188   "Never before," "In every case," Dawidowicz, "The Holocaust as Historical Record," *Dimensions of the Holocaust,* Northwestern University, Evanston, Ill., 1977, p. 32.

16. THE FINISH

189   "We were free," *Response* magazine, Simon Wiesenthal Center.

191   "Many died," Gilbert, *Atlas of the Holocaust,* p. 236.

192–193   "We had known," Abzug, *Inside the Vicious Heart,* p. 19.

17. JUSTICE

199   "I have never," Hoess, Affidavit, Cybary of the Holocaust. Internet Site.

199   "Did you prefer," to come.

18. THE TIME IS NOW

213	"The world," *Facing History*, p. 313.
217	"to be a wake-up," ADL Audit of Antisemitic Incidents 1999, Anti-Defamation League Internet site.
220	"However this war," Levi, *The Drowned and the Saved*, p. 11.
223	"the result," Jäckel, *World View*, p. 61.
223	"There is nothing," to come.
223	"Once I am really," Furet, *Unanswered Questions*, p. 107, n. 16.
229	"The Nazis came," *Facing History*, p. 206.
229	"All that it takes," Wiesel, *Night*, to come.

SELECTED TIME LINE

1933

January 30	Adolf Hitler appointed chancellor of Germany
February 28	Emergency Powers Decree
March 22	Dachau, first concentration camp, begins operation
March 24	Enabling Act
April 1	Boycott of Jewish businesses and shops
April 7	"Aryan Law." Jews expelled from civil service
May 10	Books of "un-German spirit" burned
September 29	Jews prohibited from owning land
December 18	Jews forbidden to be journalists

1934

January 24	Jews banned from German labor organization
May 17	Jews denied national health insurance

1935

May 21	Jews banned from military
August 2	Hitler becomes führer of nation
September 15	Nuremberg Laws pass

1936

March	SS Death's Head Brigade established as concentration camp guards
September 17	Heinrich Himmler appointed head of Gestapo

1937

January	Jews banned from most professions

1938

April 26	Jews register wealth and property
June 14	Jewish-owned businesses registered
July 23	Jews over fifteen required to carry identity cards
July 25	Jewish doctors forbidden to practice medicine
August 17	Jews required to add "Sarah" or "Israel" as middle names

September 27	Jews forbidden to practice law
October 5	Jewish passports and identity cards stamped with large red *J*
November 9	Kristallnacht
November 15	Jewish students expelled from German schools
December 3	Jewish businesses taken over by German citizens

1939

February 21	Jews turn in all silver and gold items
April 30	Jews relocated into "Jewish houses"
July 4	Jews forbidden to hold government-related jobs
September 1	Nazis invade Poland, World War II begins
September 1	Jewish curfew established in Germany
September 21	Reinhard Heydrich, chief of Reich Security Main Office, issues order for establishment of Jewish ghettos in occupied territory
September 23	German Jews forbidden to own radios
November 23	Polish Jews over ten required to wear Yellow Star
December	Adolf Eichmann placed in charge of Gestapo section IVB-4, the Jewish affairs department

1940

April 30	Lodz ghetto sealed off
November	Cracow ghetto sealed off
November 15	Warsaw ghetto sealed off

1941

March 7	German Jews ordered into forced labor
June 22	Germany invades Soviet Union
July	Special Action Groups begin activities in Soviet Union
July	Ghettos established in Kovno, Minsk, Vitebsk, and Zhitomer
July 31	Reichmarshall Herman Goering orders Heydrich to organize plans for Final Solution
August	Ghettos established in Lvov and Bialystok
September	Mobile gassing vans begin operation
September 1	German Jews ordered to wear Yellow Star
September 3	First test of Zyklon B at Auschwitz
September 6	Vilna ghetto established
October 23	Jews forbidden to leave Germany
November 24	Theresienstadt ghetto established
December 8	Chelmno death camp begins operation

1942

January 20	Conference at Wannsee to coordinate Final Solution
February	Mass killings using Zyklon B begin at Auschwitz
March	Belzec death camp begins operation

April 20	German Jews banned from public transportation
June 1	Jews in Holland, France, Belgium, Croatia, Romania and Slovakia ordered to wear Yellow Star
June 4	Reinhard Heydrich dies after Czech underground attack
July 19	Supreme leader of the SS Heinrich Himmler orders Operation Reinhard, the killing of all Jews in Poland
July 23	Treblinka death camp begins operation
September	Maidanek death camp begins operation
October 5	Himmler orders Jews in German concentration camps to be sent to Maidanek and Auschwitz
December	Belzec ceases operation

1943

March 14	Cracow ghetto liquidated
Spring	Commando 1005—Operation Blotout—begins
April 19	Warsaw ghetto uprising begins
May 16	Warsaw ghetto liquidated
June 11	Himmler orders liquidation of all ghettos in occupied Poland
August 2	Revolt at Treblinka
August 16	Bialystok ghetto liquidated
August	Exterminations cease at Treblinka
September	Vilna and Minsk ghettos liquidated
October 14	Revolt at Sobibor
October	Exterminations cease at Sobibor
November	Riga ghetto liquidated
November 3	Operation Harvest Festival

1944

August 6	Lodz ghetto liquidated
October 7	Revolt at Auschwitz
November 25	Himmler orders destruction of Auschwitz crematoriums

1945

1945	Death marches of concentration camp inmates toward Germany
April 30	Hitler commits suicide
May 8	Unconditional surrender of Germany
November 20	Opening of the International Military Tribunal at Nuremberg

PHOTO CREDITS

Every effort has been made to locate each owner of the photographs printed in this book to secure the necessary permissions. If there is any question regarding the use of these materials, corrections will be made in future editions.

AP/Wide World Photos: pp. 180, 229

Leo Baeck Institute: pp. xviii, 3, 12, 22, 74

Black Star: p. 214 (bottom)

Corbis: p. 151; Bettmann/Corbis: p. 158; Corbis/Owen Franken: p. 214 (top); Hulton-Deutsch Collection/Corbis: p. 19

Dimitar Dilkoff/Reuters/Getty Images: p. 219

Dorot Jewish Division, The New York Public Library, Astor, Lenox and Tilden Foundation: endpapers

Marion Pritchard: p. 169 (top)

Franklin D. Roosevelt Library and Museum: p. 150

Ruth Segal: p. 172 (both)

Stock Photo/Owen: p. 14

Harry S. Truman Library and Museum: p. 197 (bottom)

United States Holocaust Memorial Museum (USHMM): Archiwum Akt Nowych, p. 49 (detail); Glowna Komisja Badania Zbrodni Narodowi Polskiemu, p.127; Louis Gonda, p. 128–129; Hessiches Haupstaatsarchiv Wiesbaden, p. 47; KZ Gedenkstatte Dachau, p. 143 (detail); Library of Congress, p. 20; Hanne Liebmann, p. 174; Main Commission for the Prosecution of the Crimes Against the Polish Nation, p. 50 (detail); National Archives, pp. 58 (detail), 108–109 (detail); State Archives of the Russian Federation, p. 192 (detail); USHMM, pp. 6, 24, 86, 126 (detail), 140, 145 (detail), 195 (top), 196; Yad Vashem Photo Archives, p. 122

Raoul Wallenberg Committee of the United States: p. 175

Simon Wiesenthal Center Library and Archives: pp. 7, 8, 13, 21, 32, 62 (detail), 117, 170, 171, 173 (detail), 200, 202 (detail)

Yad Vashem: pp. 17, 18, 26, 29 (both), 31, 33 (both), 35, 41, 45, 46, 52, 57, 69, 75, 82, 83, 84–85, 89, 96, 99, 107, 118 (both), 130, 131, 138, 139, 164, 189, 191, 192, 193 (detail),195 (bottom), 197 (top), 204

YIVO Institute for Jewish Research: pp. 11, 23, 25, 30, 34, 37, 38, 43, 66, 70, 72, 73, 76, 79, 80, 100, 157

INDEX

לי ענת וגם שרשי ב

קשי כי השאיר שרש

זכור מ עשה אגג מערמה נשים

כשכלה חרב לענות

סורס שארי לשסות יעטה

זכור נ ניר לחומיל החסבים סר

סכים

יד לסכים

זכור ס בב בחלג ובגב עמלק

תרי

שוב הואי מצשה בעוב

זכור ע ריזן בעמוניס נחבא פריז

כרמי עז גרי כהזכא יצורכו

איש באחיו בחרב להומה

זכור פ לטים אשר בזת השעיר

יצאו בלכתם אל הר שעיר

קא לנסוב עירות שעיר

זכור צ ג בפרק להסגיר שרידי קם

באש הדבכים סעיר את הוד

דת ומסר בידם פרוד

זכור ק פז לשער השמים רעש

ושואג מי לי בשמים שלט

ויגדל עד יצבא השמים